MW01088705

Bold Ruler

Bold Ruler

by EDWARD L. BOWEN

Lexington, Kentucky

Library of Congress Control Number: 2005920847

ISBN-13: 978-1-58150-130-8
ISBN-10: 1-58150-130-7

Printed in the United States
First Edition: 2005

Distributed to the trade by
National Book Network
4501 Forbes Boulevard, Suite 200
Lanham, MD 20706
1.800.462.6420

a division of
The Blood-Horse Publications
PUBLISHERS SINCE 1916

Bold Ruler

Contents

Bold Ruler

CHAPTER 1

"Look in favor upon a bold beginning"

—Virgil

August 1956 found Whitney Tower avidly scanning the present for hints of the future. *Sports Illustrated* was barely to its second anniversary when Tower, its articulate horse racing guy, prepared for publication a commentary on the present crop of two-year-olds: "The safest place to look for your best two-year-old is to look for the most fashionable breeding among the young colts and fillies who have already won a few races this season ... If any of these has got to be singled out for special honors before he has passed even the vaguest semblance of a stamina test, that colt must be Bold Ruler, winner of all five of his races. Bold Ruler is a son of Nasrullah (the sire of Nashua) out of a Discovery mare — a combination of bloodlines that is nearly impossible to fault …"

Early on, then, one of the themes of Bold Ruler's life as a racehorse was comparison to Nashua, with its implied question of who was better. Nashua was a four-year-old at the time, and while his theretofore nearly spotless reputation was being whittled a bit by some stunning failures, he enjoyed the reputation carved by his two-year-old championship of 1954 and Horse of the Year status of 1955. In addition to sharing the same sire, the young and lean and elegantly sassy Bold Ruler shared the same trainer, one James E. "Sunny Jim" Fitzsimmons, an American success story who long since had bedraggled racing writers' supply of superlatives.

By season's end, Bold Ruler had suffered a confusing comeuppance, but the most glamorous moment of the year linked him with Nashua in a day for history: On October 13, Nashua bid farewell to racing by winning his second Jockey Club Gold Cup, passing the baton to Bold Ruler, who triumphed that same day in the grail of juvenile races of the time, the Belmont Futurity.

Bold Ruler was bred and owned by Wheatley Stable, whose mistress was Mrs. Henry Carnegie (Gladys) Phipps. Nashua was a homebred of a similarly productive breeding operation, Belair Stud, founded by William Woodward Sr. a few years before the formation of Wheatley Stable. Fitzsimmons trained for both operations for three decades or more. That he was free to seek and fulfill the crisscrossing, competitive ambitions of both can be recognized as tribute to his own character as well as to the sporting principles of the owners. Imagine a baseball manager telling his owner: "Sorry you didn't win the World Series, but I did — with one of the other teams I manage." Yet, the parallel of such a possibility is routine in Thoroughbred racing.

Even without the here-we-go-again implications of following Nashua by two years, the fledgling Bold Ruler would have been enthralling. Fitzsimmons had him ready for his debut on April 9, 1956, at the old New York track named Jamaica, a sort of egg-shaped affair that seemed to engender more sentiment after its demise than during its years of activity. Ted Atkinson was aboard, and Bold Ruler tracked the early pace and then took charge, defeating Wolf Badge by three and a half lengths. The time for five furlongs was 1:00 2/5.

Sunny Jim Fitzsimmons believed in getting a horse to the starting gate more than getting him onto the

workout list. Ten days later, Bold Ruler and Atkinson raced head and head with Red Cadet through most of a five-furlong allowance race at Jamaica and then drew out to win by a length. "Ridden out" was the description in the *Daily Racing Form* chart. During the race, Bold Ruler veered enough that Red Cadet's rider claimed foul, but the order stood. The time was 1:00. Third was a colt named Missile, whose own early impression had trumped that of Bold Ruler to the extent that he was the odds-on choice. Both Missile and fourth-placed Clem were destined for distinction and additional confrontations with Bold Ruler.

On May 2, less than a month after his debut, Bold Ruler moved into stakes company to contest the Youthful Stakes in his third start. Coupled with Wheatley's Supernatural in an even-money entry, Bold Ruler was away tardily but soon took up the fray in battling again with Red Cadet. He drew out to win by three and a half lengths in :59 4/5. Red Cadet again was second, and Encore was third. Spanish San, who had raced five furlongs in :59 while winning his debut, was scratched with bucked shins.

"He's still a little green," Atkinson said of Bold

Ruler after the race, "but he seems to be learning every time."

Racing then moved to Belmont Park, and Eddie Arcaro, "the Master," replaced Atkinson as Bold Ruler's rider. Arcaro, who also rode Nashua for Fitzsimmons, would be aboard for all but three of Bold Ruler's remaining thirty starts. Down the old, straight Widener chute came Bold Ruler in a May 24 allowance race, with the early Florida stakes winner King Hairan battling him fiercely. Bold Ruler won by a neck. Time for five furlongs on the straight course was :57 1/5. "All out" was the chart comment.

The Juvenile Stakes came up next, on June 6, and again found the Wheatley colt facing King Hairan at five furlongs down the Widener Chute. The Juvenile had been first run in 1874, and while June of a juvenile season is early to begin thinking of future classics, a few who had won it went on to greater glory at the races or in the stud. Among them were Tremont, Broomstick, Blue Larkspur, Equipoise, My Request, and Nashua.

At equal weight of 122 pounds, King Hairan took off to gain the lead and had one and a half lengths on Bold

Ruler after a half-mile in :44 1/5. With only a furlong remaining, Arcaro gunned Bold Ruler and the colt took over quickly enough to convince the *Form* chart caller that his one-length victory found him "in hand." The time of :56 was only one-fifth away from the Widener chute record for five furlongs and was four-fifths of a second swifter than Polly's Jet's stakes record, set the previous year.

So, Bold Ruler had won five in a row and was the pro-tem leader of the division, albeit, as Tower noted, it was very early to begin drawing conclusions or making plans.

CHAPTER 2

A Sense Of Sport And Elegance

Mrs. Henry Carnegie Phipps and Sunny Jim Fitzsimmons had raced just such a promising two-year-old before, and sobering experience went hand in hand with the optimism of expectation.

Early in their owner-trainer connection had come another dashing youngster, unbeaten as the spring wound into summer. This was Dice, one of a remarkable draft of eight horses Mrs. Phipps had acquired from Harry Payne Whitney that established Wheatley as a force in Eastern racing with one fell swoop.

No question, Dice was a quick one. Like Bold Ruler, Dice (Dominant—Frumpery, by Chicle) ripped off five victories from five starts in the spring and early summer of 1927, and one race in his streak, too, was the Juvenile. The others included the Hudson Stakes, Keene Memorial, and Great American, in which he gave twenty pounds to Sun Edwin. (W. Averell Harriman soon afterward gave $75,000 to buy Sun Edwin.)

Then, suddenly, the comet named Dice fell to earth. At Saratoga later that summer, he suffered an internal hemorrhage and died.

"I have handled many horses in my time," Fitzsimmons said at the time, "and have seen thousands of them perform, but only one horse in my memory had all the characteristics which Dice displayed, and that was Exterminator." (Readers of *The Black Stallion* and viewers of the movie based on the book should have no trouble connecting this bit of history to author Walter Farley's crusty old fictional character Henry Dailey and his nostalgia over his long-lamented star, Hash.)

So, the bold beginning of Wheatley Stable had been tempered by merciless, random fate.

Although Mrs. Phipps was new as an owner of a racing stable, she almost certainly was not surprised that even the best horses, given the best care, would not be immune to misfortune or mischance. She had been around horses all her life. A photo in the *Illustrated*

Sporting News of September 19, 1903, shows her as a wisp of a young lady, riding sidesaddle in the Newport Horse Show, looking down intently at her mount from beneath a flat, brimmed hat. In that photo of the show ring, the dainty "Miss Gladys Mills" and her mount are flanked by the more imposing figures of Mrs. W.E. Woodend and Miss Marion Fish on their own steeds.

Gladys Mills represented a confluence of two admirably achieving families in American life. Her mother was Ruth Livingston, which meant she traced to "a fortune that had its origin in a royal grant from the British Crown," according to Bernard Livingston's *Their Turf* (Arbor House, New York, 1973). The family arrived in the New World in 1674 in the person of Robert Livingston, who was born in Scotland but had lived in Rotterdam. Livingston married well and soon acquired 160,000 acres from the British Crown.

Livingstons of later generations, according to *Their Turf,* slipped their moorings from the Crown and "signed the Declaration of Independence ... held a monopoly on steamboating on the Hudson River, and ... displayed expertise ... in handling of the Louisiana Purchase negotiations for the U.S. Government."

On her father's side, Gladys Mills sprung from a similarly although more recent, saga of upward striving and achievement. Her paternal grandfather, Darius Ogden Mills, was born in North Salem, New York, in 1825. His father was a banker but died when the son was sixteen, and his father's recent investments had proven so ineffectual that Darius Ogden Mills was later quoted to the effect that "I was taught very early that I would have to depend entirely upon myself, that my future was in my own hands."

Mills handled that future adroitly. He went one better than the eager hunters of riches converging on northern California during the gold rush. He followed them and established businesses supplying the gold miners and their camps with essentials. This led to establishing a bank (presumably for the most successful of the forty-niners), and he was so successful that the phrase "the luck of D.O. Mills" was said to have worked its way into local parlance. Mills founded the Bank of San Francisco in 1864, survived a roller coaster few years of that institution, and emerged with sufficient wherewithal to move back to his Eastern roots and erect the largest office building in New York.

Another quotation attributed to Mills was: "A knowledge of men is the prime secret of business success." Whatever were the secondary secrets, he seemed to grasp them as well.

In addition to thriving enterprise and philanthropy back East, Mills commissioned extensive renovations to the family's upstate New York home, Staatsburg, which his wife's great-grandfather had purchased in 1792.

In one final accomplishment, Darius Ogden Mills, the man who had moved mountains in a figurative sense, had a real mountain named for him. He had been a founder and charter member of the Sierra Club, and after his death in 1910, the club successfully promoted the idea of naming a 13,468-foot California formation Mount Mills.

Darius Ogden Mills' son, Ogden Mills, was involved in launching the family into Thoroughbred racing. He formed a transatlantic partnership with the leading English Thoroughbred owner and breeder of the day, Lord Derby. While Lord Derby's breeding and racing in England was a personal affair, he joined Mills in a French stable partnership. This partnership was the leading owner in France in 1928, when Lord Derby's and Mills' Kantar won the Prix de l'Arc de Triomphe and Cri de Guerre won the Grand Prix de Paris.

That distinction came three years after one of Ogden Mills' three children, the aforementioned Gladys, had dipped into the Saratoga Thoroughbred market to buy three yearlings, the prices being $8,000, $7,500, and $1,600. None distinguished itself.

Ogden Mills passed away in 1929, leaving a son, Ogden Livingston Mills, as well as twin daughters, Gladys and Beatrice.

Gladys Livingston Mills, granddaughter of Darius Ogden Mills and daughter of Ogden Mills, was born in Newport, Rhode Island, on June 19, 1883, but grew up at Staatsburg. (She gave the home to the state of New York after it passed to her years later.) In 1907, in her mid-twenties, Gladys Mills married Henry Carnegie Phipps.

As any schoolchild might glean from the name Carnegie, this represented another blending of prominently achieving American heritage. Henry Carnegie Phipps' father, Henry Phipps, was the son of a Scottish cobbler and lived in Allegheny, Pennsylvania, during the 1840s. Henry Phipps became friends with Andrew Carnegie, son of a similarly struggling family, and some years later that friendship resulted in Carnegie inviting his childhood friend to support him in an investment. Carnegie had an opportunity to buy a forge at Girty's Run, and, as has often been told, Phipps' eight hundred dollar investment and his acumen at bookkeeping and labor control translated into $50 million when Carnegie sold the firm — by then known as Carnegie Steel Company — nearly forty years later to J.P. Morgan (U.S. Steel) for $250 million.

Henry Phipps went about giving to so many causes of the common man that Carnegie was quoted that he was "spoiling humanity," but Phipps was no fool. Phipps lived into his nineties and provided for the ongoing success of his family via Bessemer Trust as well as dispensing largesse to the masses.

He was survived by two daughters and three sons, one of whom, as described earlier, was Henry Carnegie Phipps, husband of Gladys Livingston Mills.

When Gladys, Mrs. Henry Carnegie Phipps, decided to venture into Thoroughbred racing, she used the name Wheatley Stable. Wheatley was the name of a road on which the Phippses' home in Westbury, Long Island, was situated. Ogden Phipps, son of Mr. and Mrs. Henry Carnegie Phipps, told us in a 1989 interview that he felt his own interest in racing encouraged his mother to become involved. He added that his father "did not much care for racing, although he was a polo player and hunted some in England." Henry Carnegie Phipps was involved in real estate development and finance.

Mrs. Phipps recruited her brother, Ogden Livingston Mills, to be her partner. Her brother's time was rather well spoken for at the moment, inasmuch as he was the undersecretary of the treasury to Andrew Mellon. In 1932 Mills was named to succeed Mellon as secretary of the treasury by Herbert Hoover's administration.

Three failed yearlings do not a dynasty foretell. Conversely, perhaps a card game does.

Well, probably not, for three of Mrs. Phipps' grandchildren told the author they had never heard of the tale set out as fact in *Their Turf*. Nevertheless, the story is too delightful to go untold, although festooned with disclaimers. Author Livingston's book describes Gladys Mills Phipps' deus ex machina as feminine opportunism responding to a pair of manly preoccupations, e.g., gambling and late nights. By this telling, the key Eastern Thoroughbred owner Harry Payne Whitney lost a packet at cards to Henry Carnegie Phipps and offered to pay off in bloodstock — yearlings, to be specific. The following morning, Phipps showed up to collect the debt and was waved to the stables by Whitney, he secure in the knowledge that Phipps was a novice when it came to Thoroughbreds. Whitney failed to notice that the diminutive Gladys Phipps was also in the limousine, however, and it was she who picked through the sprightly young Whitney stock.

Cynthia Phipps, Ogden Mills Phipps, and Stuart Janney III each individually expressed bewilderment that such a story could be circulated. Phipps went so far as to say he did not remember his grandfather ever playing cards and that his grandparents "were not gamblers."

The more commonly reported version over the years, the one Ogden Mills Phipps grew up knowing, was that Harry Payne Whitney, who was a close friend, wanted to help Mrs. Phipps get established in the sport and did so by giving her the opportunity to choose

from among his yearling crop.

This more supportable and familiar version nevertheless is consistent with the proposition that it was Mrs. Phipps' shrewd horsemanship that was brought to bear on the opportunity, and she did not let opportunity slink away. In addition to the brilliant Dice, those she plucked to race in the Wheatley colors included Jockey Club Gold Cup winner Diavolo, Wood Memorial winner Distraction, and Alabama Stakes winner Nixie!

Mrs. Phipps' son, Ogden Phipps, said he always presumed that it was the influence of William Woodward Sr., whose Belair Stud's star was also in the ascendant, that connected Mrs. Phipps to the Hancock family's Claiborne Farm in Kentucky as a base for the Wheatley breeding stock. It was not Woodward, however, but J.E. Davis, a friend of Mrs. Phipps and a steward of The Jockey Club, who connected her with one James E. Fitzsimmons to train her racehorses, although Fitzsimmons already had the Belair connection, having signed on to train the Woodward stable a few years earlier.

The three — Fitz, Phipps, and Woodward — were to

forge an enduring chapter in Thoroughbred racing that stands today as a guidepost to those who seek from the Turf a sense of sport and elegance, linked with competition and good sense.

In the nearly three decades between Dice and Bold Ruler, Wheatley Stable's majestic silks of golden yellow, purple sleeves, and purple cap had many a major score:

Homebred Edelweiss won a key filly race, the Coaching Club American Oaks in 1933; Dark Secret won two Jockey Club Gold Cups (1933–34); Snark won the time-honored Metropolitan and Suburban handicaps in 1937 and 1938, respectively, amid a rush of stakes triumphs; Teufel and Melodist won back-to-back Wood Memorials in the late 1930s; Merry Lassie won the 1937 Spinaway and Matron; Hostility won the 1939 Acorn; High Voltage was 1954 champion two-year-old filly and the 1955 Coaching Club American Oaks winner, and then was beaten out for the three-year-old filly championship that year by none other than her Wheatley stablemate Misty Morn.

On the negative side, Seabiscuit was sold off and became a champion and an American icon carrying

other silks; Dark Secret was injured so badly in his second Gold Cup that he could not be saved; and droughts of victory — ever a part of the Turf — were from time to time visited upon the stable.

In the more personal aspects of a life's journey, Mrs. Phipps' brother Ogden Livingston Mills died in 1937 and husband Henry Carnegie Phipps (who in time had become more involved in racing) died in 1953, just a year before a series of champions would appear. In the face of each loss, Mrs. Phipps determined to carry on Wheatley Stable.

"My grandmother was very involved with her horses," recalled grandson Ogden Mills "Dinny" Phipps, the present chairman of The Jockey Club. Mrs. Phipps would load a pair of poodles into her Bentley and drive herself to the racetrack several mornings a week to visit her horses and talk racing with Fitzsimmons. (She was a resident of Florida, so would have attended racing at Hialeah during the winter, and then she spent part of the year in New York, where the Wheatley horses were headquartered in spring, summer, and early autumn.) "She did her own breeding list," Phipps continued. "She discussed it with Bull (Hancock of

Claiborne Farm) and my father (Ogden Phipps), but she did it herself first. She also kept her own books and paid her own bills for the stable."

One of Mrs. Phipps' three daughters, Mrs. Sonia Seherr-Thoss, recalled in 2005 that, "It must have been in the later 1950s when my mother once remarked to me that 'never in any one year have I lost money in racing.' "

A constant element of the stable for many years, of course, was that Wheatley's trainer was Sunny Jim Fitzsimmons.

"The only time she ever made a speech was at Belmont Park," in the old horseman's honor, Mrs. Seherr-Thoss recalled. "I asked if she had what she was going to say written down, and she said, 'No, I'll remember what to say.' She was in her seventies and making her first speech, and she did it very well."

"She had a wonderful relationship with Mr. Fitzsimmons," Dinny Phipps recalled. "She called him 'Fitz.' It was hard for her when Mr. Fitz retired (1963), but she had a good relationship (afterward) with Bill Winfrey and then Eddie Neloy. It goes back to her loving her horses."

Mrs. Phipps apparently was not of the ilk to seek publicity. Consequently, the few interviews she gave tended to be placed in publications' files and brought up from time to time as reference. Over the years journalists leaped upon a quotation attributed to her in the *New York World Telegram* in 1939: "It isn't winning the races. That isn't it. It's entering a horse in a race and knowing he will do the best he can. I do not care too much about winning the race ... It's just that I want them to perform like the Thoroughbreds they are. That is the important thing."

Well, the present writer read this back to her son, Ogden, during an interview fifty years later and received a quizzical and abrupt response: "Where'd you find that? Of course, she wanted to win."

Nevertheless, Mrs. Seherr-Thoss recalled that her mother's approach could be summarized as, "If they won that was wonderful. If they didn't ... oh, well."

Dinny Phipps' sister Cynthia recalled of their grandmother during a run of major success in the 1960s that, "I would say she was pretty competitive, but it was a generational thing that she just wouldn't show it. She was such a lady that you could hardly have perceived from the exterior how pleased she was. She enjoyed the horses, and she would bet twenty dollars on them — never more, never less. The better they did the more pleased she was, but there was this 'old-fashioned' control.

"She got an intense pleasure from her racing stable, and she loved naming them," Cynthia added. "She was very good at naming horses."

Cynthia Phipps also recalled that Mrs. Phipps "was a competitive golfer and loved to play bridge. She was a very good player and she played with people who were serious about bridge. In the early days she also did a lot of shooting, grouse and pheasant, in Scotland and was a fine fly-fisherman. She went up to the Great Cascapedia River in Canada and would use these heavy wooden rods to go fly-casting, although she was a very small lady." Dinny Phipps shared the same vision, recalling "in the days before graphite rods they used fourteen-foot-long wooden fly rods, which she handled very well."

Mrs. Seherr-Thoss remembered her mother as being "a beautiful rider, and she was an extremely good golfer. She used to play with the really top ladies." The

interest in sports passed down to her children and, the daughter recalled, "She would come to watch us do whatever we did. I played both golf and tennis but was sort of the 'also-ran.' Ogden for many years was the national court tennis champion."

After the death of Mrs. Phipps' husband, Cynthia conjectured, her grandmother's outdoor activities were not prevalent, and "the stable took over her interest more and more."

In the first two years after Henry Carnegie Phipps' death, Wheatley had raced the champions High Voltage and Misty Morn. Yet, glory's siren song was not yet in full melody.

CHAPTER 3

"In youth...hearts touched with fire"

—Oliver Wendell Holmes Jr.

If five victories from the first five starts by Bold Ruler at two caused Gladys Phipps and Sunny Jim Fitzsimmons to recall the good times of a Dice told tale, there was soon to be a reminder of the downside of having a brilliant two-year-old. Happily, Bold Ruler's setbacks were neither permanent nor tragic but were among serial maladies that would trouble a colt who for the most part seemed graced and blessed.

The problems had started at birth. A.B. Hancock Jr., the master of Claiborne Farm, where the Phipps horses were born and raised, thought back later to the young Bold Ruler and remembered "a very skinny foal with a large hernia. We had the devil's own time trying to get him to look good, and I must say, I was never really pleased with his condition the whole time I had him."

Then, as a yearling, Bold Ruler apparently fought the chain that routinely links a horse from the halter to a screw-eye in the stall wall when he is being readied for training. Bold Ruler lacerated his tongue severely and the sensitivity resulting from that mishap later was said perhaps to have cost him a victory in no less than the Kentucky Derby!

In the spring of 1956, the menu of problems resumed when Bold Ruler slammed into the gate at the start of the Juvenile Stakes, hurting his back. Then a hock problem decreed that he would miss the revered Saratoga August meeting, and, for a time, caused the trainer to wonder if the colt would get back to the races at all that year. Fitzsimmons had first encountered Saratoga as a jockey in 1893 — "I rode William T. in the Flash. He finished second, and it might have been my fault." Beginning with Nashua's and High Voltage's juvenile campaigns in 1954, Mr. Fitz had at least one champion or championship candidate on his hands for five consecutive years. Nashua won the Grand Union Hotel Stakes and Hopeful Stakes at two and Misty Morn won the Diana at three in 1955. Otherwise the Saratoga meetings were vacant for Mr. Fitz's stars, and various matters conspired against the trainer even running either Nashua or Bold Ruler at the old Spa track in any of their subsequent campaigns.

In the case of Bold Ruler at two, there was a gap of three and a half months between the Juvenile and his comeback in the autumn. On September 24, Bold Ruler reappeared at Belmont Park for a six-furlong prep for the Futurity Stakes and, despite the layoff, he was odds-on to win under 122 pounds. In the interim, on September 8, he had worked three furlongs in :32 4/5, pulling up a half-mile in :47 2/5.

Bold Ruler's penchant for problems continued. In the Futurity prep, he slammed his head on the gate and came back bleeding from the mouth, having suffered his first loss. Reports indicated he "bore out" during the running. Apparently, Bold Ruler veered and dropped back when Arcaro went to the whip, and he wound up beaten one and a quarter lengths by Nashville, another son of Nasrullah.

On October 5, Bold Ruler came out again, for the Anticipation Purse, six furlongs down the Widener Chute. Arcaro had been called to France, for owner C.V. Whitney's sporting go at the Prix de l'Arc de Triomphe with Fisherman and Career Boy. (Arcaro finished fourth on Career Boy, behind the unbeaten Ribot.) Eric Guerin got the call on Bold Ruler, and the colt, a 9-10 favorite, ran straight and true, winning by a half-length over Missile in 1:08 3/5. As an historical footnote, the beaten field included Nearctic, Cohoes, and Iron Liege. Thus, unknowingly, the Belmont Park crowd that day saw one of the greatest of future stallions (Bold Ruler); the sire of a comparable stallion (Nearctic, sire of Northern Dancer); the sire of a future Belmont Stakes winner (Cohoes, sire of Quadrangle) and the next year's Kentucky Derby winner (Iron Liege).

The Futurity was October 13, the day four-year-old Nashua won his second Jockey Club Gold Cup in his farewell to racing. Bold Ruler came out a half-hour later as the 6-5 favorite for the Futurity. Nearctic dashed a quarter-mile down the straight course in :21 4/5, and then Arcaro — reunited with Bold Ruler — sent the favorite into top gear, and they opened a three-length lead. At the finish, Bold Ruler had a two-length margin over Greek Game in 1:15 1/5 for six and a half furlongs. The time had been bettered only by Native Dancer and Blue Peter. The *New York Times* quoted a satisfied Arcaro: "It was the easiest ride I ever had on this horse."

Sports Illustrated's Whitney Tower quoted Arcaro's further explanation that Bold Ruler was "suddenly a different colt than I'd ever known him to be. He's usually bad at the gate and fidgety getting to it. Today he was loose and limber as a dishrag on the way up and then perfectly behaved at the start."

Arcaro was pressed by Tower to comment on the retiring four-year-old Nashua and the free-running heir apparent:

"I wouldn't want to start comparing him to Nashua yet," he said of Bold Ruler, "but one difference between the two is that when you move on Bold Ruler he'll go by and beat anything up front. He likes to win and doesn't have to be driven to it."

No owner of racehorses could resist a Bold Ruler — a homebred of brilliance today that gives off the headiest prospects for tomorrow.

"She did have her favorites, and she just adored Bold Ruler," Cynthia Phipps told us of her grandmother Gladys Phipps. The colt further seduced his aging owner with a most endearing trait. "He loved

sugar, and when you gave him sugar he would always put one front foot on your foot," Cynthia added. "He wouldn't hurt you, but he'd just reach out with one foot and put it on yours."

After the Futurity, the *Times* nonchalantly referred to Bold Ruler as "the champion 2-year-old," without qualification. In truth, the juvenile championship presumably had been won but only if accepted on the terms of that afternoon.

On the one hand, the six and a half-furlong Futurity had been long recognized as the most important two-year-old race. However, there was also a history of autumn races as long as one and one-sixteenth miles for juveniles, and to some observers these longer races were regarded as the more important indicators of classic potential at three.

By Bold Ruler's day, the juvenile picture had undergone a recent sea change. Three years before, in 1953, Gene Mori had made the Garden State Stakes — one and one-sixteenth miles for two-year-olds in the autumn — not only the richest race for juveniles, but also the richest race for any age group in the world. In 1953 Turn-to had won the first running of the super-rich event, earning more than $150,000. (As a means of comparison, Turn-to's owner, Captain Harry Guggenheim's Cain Hoy Stable, had earned $90,050 from Dark Star's victory in the Kentucky Derby earlier that year.)

In 1956 it is probably fair to say that Bold Ruler's campaign — and the lingering prestige of the old Futurity — would have carried the day in *Daily Racing Form* and Thoroughbred Racing Associations championship balloting had he pranced safely off into winter quarters. The Phipps operation, however, has never been one to duck a challenge — traditional or not.

Thus, Bold Ruler was sent out for the Garden State Stakes at Garden State Park in New Jersey on October 27, two weeks after the Futurity. In a field of nineteen, he was sent off the favorite at slightly more than 2-1. Arcaro had been suspended for an infraction at Keeneland in Kentucky, and Atkinson, Bold Ruler's springtime jockey, was reunited with the colt.

There was plenty of speed in the Garden State, with Bold Ruler and the flyer Federal Hill, but a two-time stakes winner from Detroit, Jaunty John, tore off in front, opening five lengths while traversing a half-mile in :45 4/5. He then dropped back so suddenly that Bold Ruler — poised along the rail — ran into his heels, nearly falling. Thereafter, the richest race in the world was a non-entity for Bold Ruler, who fell back to finish seventeenth as Calumet Farm's Barbizon came on to edge Federal Hill by a nose.

Scuttled, but unscathed, Bold Ruler appeared once more that autumn, but he did not help his cause. He was 3-5 as a crowd of 40,518 turned out at Jamaica for the November 6 Remsen Stakes, which again tested juveniles at one and one-sixteenth miles. He finished last.

He had been troublesome at the gate, and Arcaro later noted to the *New York Times* that, "He took a step at the gate, but I had to snatch him back when it wasn't a start. If we had kept going then, he would have been in front on the first turn … As it was, he was tight all the rest of the way. He didn't respond to the whip when I started at the half-mile pole, and he ran beyond my comprehension. I can't explain it. Something must be hurting him — even though he pulled up all right — to do as bad as that."

Fitzsimmons had been planning to run Bold Ruler

in the Pimlico Futurity, also at a mile and one-sixteenth, but decided to stop for the year. Bold Ruler thus had a season's record of seven wins in ten races and earnings of $139,050.

The trainer, like the rider, found the situation incomprehensible: "There's absolutely nothing wrong with him that I can find, but I think I'll wait until next year with him rather than keep him in training. He'll go to Hialeah with the rest of the horses after the New York season closes — sometime between Nov. 15 and Nov. 20."

Fitzsimmons elaborated for the *Times,* on his bafflement over the Remsen performance: "I can't explain it, and he can't talk to me and tell me what happened. So, I guess we'll have to go along with what we saw. He was almost eliminated from the race at the start and got a pretty good bumping on the first turn. When Eddie got him to the outside down the backstretch, the colt just would not run. Maybe he hurt himself a little around the turn and decided not to run after that." Sunny Jim concluded his comments with a statement that spoke to the heart of being a trainer, wrapped up in the well-being as well as the perfor-

mance of his horses: "He came back to me at the barn all right."

Voters had to scratch their heads. Here was a brilliant colt, consistent to a fault, until his last two races, winner of the time-honored Futurity and other good stakes. And yet, he had been seventeenth and eleventh as a conclusion to his campaign. On the other hand, there was Barbizon, carrying the glorious colors of Calumet Farm. True, he had won only one stakes, but it was the richest race in the world, and he had won a total of five of six races and was finishing strongly at the end of one and one-sixteenth miles.

Barbizon got the nod on both the *Daily Racing Form* and Thoroughbred Racing Associations polls. Racing secretary Jimmy Kilroe, in compiling the Experimental Free Handicap for The Jockey Club, could only concur. He assigned Barbizon 126 pounds, with Bold Ruler and Federal Hill each assigned 125. Calumet had another champion. Wheatley had a puzzle.

CHAPTER 4

A Colt Of Character

Baffling performances by any son of Nasrullah invited the thought that the sire's idiosyncrasy might be nudging upward into genetic expression, and Bold Ruler was not immune to such conjecture. After all, Nasrullah was the horse who had engendered high praise in the English publication *Racehorses of 1943*, which at the same time published photos of him with such captions as "Nasrullah impersonating a mule" and "Nasrullah pretending to be a gentleman."

To those who saw him, Nasrullah was apparently a lovable rogue. His first great star after his importation, Nashua, was well known to give Arcaro fits with his lackadaisical tendencies. Thus, just as Bold Ruler inherited the flatteries implicit in comparison to Nashua, he was — perhaps unjustifiably — presumed also to have some of the other horse's negative traits.

Bred by His Highness the Aga Khan, Nasrullah was a foal of 1940 and was sired by Federico Tesio's unbeaten Nearco, a pivotal stallion of the mid-twentieth century.

Nasrullah's female family was also a study in class and prolonged influence. His dam, Mumtaz Begum, was by Blenheim II, an Epsom Derby winner who was imported to Claiborne Farm years before Nasrullah arrived. Mumtaz Begum was also the dam of Sun Princess, in turn, the dam of the major sire Royal Charger. Yet another important contemporary sire, Mahmoud, was by Blenheim II out of Mumtaz Begum's half sister, Mah Mahal.

Mumtaz Begum and Mah Mahal were out of Mumtaz Mahal, virtually always referred to as "the flying filly" both during and after her racing career. A foal of 1921, Mumtaz Mahal was by the pivotal speed sire The Tetrarch. She won seven races at two and three and topped the English Free Handicap at two in 1923.

Moreover, Mumtaz Mahal herself was backed up by earlier excellence in her female family. Her dam, Lady Josephine (by Sundridge), also produced the storied Lady Juror, dam of no fewer than eight stakes winners, including leading English sire Fair Trial.

Thus, the Nearco—Mumtaz Begum colt represented many generations of high racing class, and a family replete with important stallions in its production history. Accounts of the time indicate that he, Nasrullah, was as handsome in the flesh as on the pedigree page.

"Whatever else may be said of Nasrullah, it is clear that he is a colt of character," wrote V.R. Orchard in *The Bloodstock Breeders' Review*. "In appearance he is a rich bay of commanding proportions. His quarters are immensely powerful, and any good judge of a horse would put down this fine-looking colt as near perfect as possible if considering him apart from his racecourse performance."

That last dig was earned. At two Nasrullah ran four times, winning the Coventry Stakes and one other race while finishing second in the Middle Park Stakes, in earlier eras the Futurity's counterpart in England. He was ranked among the best colts but was weighted a pound below the Nearco filly Lady Sybil.

At three Nasrullah's "temperamental vagaries came into full flower," as horseman and historian Abe Hewitt once put it. Like Nashua would be, he could be frustrating even in victory. In the Chatteris Stakes, his first run at three, Nasrullah managed to win despite easing up considerably while in front. With his first classic engagement, the one-mile Two Thousand Guineas, next on the horizon, trainer Frank Butters resorted to blinkers — then known as "the rogue's badge" on the English Turf. They failed in the intent of keeping Nasrullah focused, for he pulled up after taking the lead and resisted champion jockey Gordon Richards' best persuasive tactics. Nasrullah allowed himself to fall back to fourth.

Next came the greatest of all prizes, the Epsom Derby. Nasrullah again went to the front but lost interest and fell back. He did get a place, finishing third behind Straight Deal and Umiddad.

While in retrospect it might seem that Nasrullah would be implanting doubt in Butters' mind relative to his stamina — as well as to his professionalism — this apparently was not the case. Butters persevered with the plan to run Nasrullah in the St. Leger, at one and three-quarters miles the longest of the English classics. In the interim, Nasrullah relented to winning a race, the one and a quarter-mile Cavensham, but in reluctant style for a 1-4 favorite. Then, in the St. Leger, he failed to make the lead and finished sixth as two fillies, Herringbone and Ribbon, defeated Derby winner Straight Deal.

Dropping back to one and a quarter miles on the straight for the Champion Stakes at Newmarket, Nasrullah regained a bit of his prestige and quite likely needed to do so to preserve the high interest he had provoked among the world's breeders. Nasrullah — and history — owe a debt to Sir Gordon Richards here, for the crafty rider had the cold nerves to wait and wait on the horse. Almost immediately after the colt had been induced to take the lead and therefore discovered it was time to let up, he had swished under the wire a length in front. It was too late to relinquish victory.

Nasrullah had won five of ten races and earned $15,240.

Back in Kentucky, Bull Hancock coveted the horse for his stallion barn. He respected the need for staying power, but he also understood the importance of speed. As he recalled years later: "I picked him out because he was the best 2-year-old (colt) of his year; he was third in the Derby, and got 1 1/4 miles very well."

Hancock was thwarted on his first attempt. He authorized the British Bloodstock Agency to offer

$50,000 for Nasrullah right out of training, but the Aga Khan had already sold him to Ireland's Joe McGrath. In 1949 Hancock took another run at Nasrullah. He, along with William Woodward Sr., Captain Harry Guggenheim, and E.P. Taylor, appeared to have the horse bought at 100,000 pounds. Taylor, a Canadian, was making the deal for them in pounds, but only days before the culmination of the deal, the pound was devalued and the transaction fell through.

In 1950 Hancock was still trying, although the horse was ten years old by then. McGrath accepted an offer of $320,000, but even then things did not go smoothly. Hancock felt he met the deadline for submission of some "earnest" money, but because of a bank holiday abroad, McGrath did not receive it in time and suggested that the option was thus nullified. In the meantime, the Hancocks always surmised, McGrath had received a larger offer, said to be from Neil McCarthy of California.

Hancock, accompanied by his wife and his father-in-law, an attorney, traveled to New York, where McGrath agreed to meet them. Although perhaps expecting enmity, Hancock and McGrath — horse guys to the core — hit it off personally and worked out a deal. The price was $340,000, with McGrath retaining a service to Nasrullah annually.

At length, the horse arrived at Claiborne Farm in the summer of 1950. By the end of the following year, Nasrullah's early bloom as a stallion had been enhanced. He ranked as the leading sire in England[1] in 1951, and his Irish-bred son Noor had reigned as 1950 champion older horse in this country with his gaudy distinction of having four consecutive wins over former Triple Crown winner Citation. Nasrullah also had sired English Oaks and Guineas winner Musidora, One Thousand Guineas winner Belle of All, Irish Derby winner Nathoo, and the accomplished Indian Hemp and Grey Sovereign.

Standing his first season at Claiborne in 1951, he got the champion Nashua in his first American-sired crop. Nashua was the first of Nasrullah's eight American-sired champions, which, with Noor, gave him a total of nine. The others, in addition to Bold Ruler, were Bald Eagle, Jaipur, Leallah, Nadir, Nasrina, and Never Bend. Also foaled in this country but raced abroad was Never Say Die, who in 1954 became the second American-bred to win the Epsom Derby.

In 1955 Nasrullah became the first stallion to have led the sire list in England and North America, and he added four more years as leading sire in this country — 1956, 1959, 1960, and 1962. (Northern Dancer later led in both countries.) Only Star Shoot and Bull Lea among twentieth-century sires in America could match five years as leader at the time, although Nasrullah's son Bold Ruler was destined to break that record.

Nasrullah stood only nine seasons at Claiborne, dying in the spring of 1959 at the age of nineteen. He sired a total of ninety-eight stakes winners (23 percent) here and abroad, and in addition to racing excellence he begot a series of important stallions to carry on the line. These included, of course, Bold Ruler, plus Nashua and Never Bend (sire of Mill Reef), from among his best racing sons. Others lower on the radar screen as racehorses also became major influences, among them Red God (sire of Blushing Groom), Grey Sovereign (sire of Caro), and Indian Hemp (sire of T. V. Lark).

Nasrullah's daughters were also revered as producers. One of them, Delta, was a Claiborne homebred who was voted Broodmare of the Year.

So, Bold Ruler sprang from a font of highest class on

the top half of his pedigree. His female family had lesser, albeit admirable, qualifications.

The dam, Miss Disco, had been bred by one of the leading sportsmen of the East, Alfred G. Vanderbilt, who had become a serious breeder and owner in the decade after Wheatley's beginnings.

Vanderbilt fell in love with Thoroughbreds and racing while a schoolboy, and upon reaching the age of twenty-one he inherited Sagamore Farm in the pleasant horse country of Maryland. He registered his colors in 1932, and the next year made a pivotal purchase in acquiring Discovery from Walter Salmon Sr. for $25,000. For the next three years, Discovery climbed the ranks of America's great horses, especially in the handicap division. Young Vanderbilt was unafraid of any racing secretary, and he allowed Discovery such achievements as three consecutive Brooklyn Handicap victories, with weights up to 136 pounds.

With a Thoroughbred farm in his ownership and an obviously high-class stallion prospect developing, Vanderbilt set about gathering a broodmare band. In 1935, when Discovery was a four-year-old, one of the leading breeders of the time, W.R. Coe, sold his

Shoshone Farm in Kentucky to horse-show enthusiast Mrs. M.F. Yount (who built Spindletop Hall on the property) and asked E.J. Tranter of Fasig-Tipton Company to conduct a dispersal at the farm. Indicative of the high quality and fashion collected by Coe was the gathering around the stallion barn at Shoshone on November 11, 1935. Such leading breeders as Colonel E.R. Bradley, Joseph E. Widener, George D. Widener, Hal Price Headley, and Samuel D. Riddle, as well as young Vanderbilt, were on site. Several of them came away with something significant to the future.

Dr. E.A. Caslick, representing a joint venture between Claiborne Farm and Charles A. and Whitney Stone, paid the top price of $20,000 for the stallion Pompey. A number of the successful stallion's thirty-one stakes winners were to be sired afterward, including his leading earner, Rippey ($299,115). For $4,600, Audley Farm of Virginia secured the young stallion Pilate, who was to sire twenty-three stakes winners, including the extraordinary runner and sire Eight Thirty and the Belmont Stakes winner Phalanx.

Among the buyers of mares, perhaps George D. Widener made the biggest score, getting Dinner Time for $6,000. She was carrying Eight Thirty, who won $155,475 in Widener's colors and proceeded to sire forty-four stakes winners. Headley paid $5,000 for Conclave, whose 1940 foal, Askmenow, would win the American Derby, Selima Stakes, Pimlico Oaks, and so on. Thomas Carr Piatt paid $3,500 for Jezebel, who six years later foaled Arlington Futurity winner Jezrahel.

A representative of Wheatley Stable was present and purchased the eight-year-old Friar Rock mare Nile Maiden, winner of two races, for $3,000. Nile Maiden later foaled two stakes-placed colts in Asp and Free Lance. In both cases, the historic Travers was among the races in which they got a piece of the purse.

Vanderbilt went to $4,000 to buy Herodias, the nineteen-year-old dam of Pilate and two other stakes winners. More germane to the tale of Bold Ruler, however, was Vanderbilt's other purchase at the Coe sale — the nine-year-old mare Sweep Out, bought for $2,000. Sweep Out was in foal to Pompey at the time. The mare's 1932 Pompey filly, Clean Out, had not yet won a stakes but would win the Escondido and San Diego handicaps at five in 1937.

Prior to joining Coe's Shoshone Stud broodmare

band, Sweep Out had won thirteen races in thirty-five starts and had earned $19,490. She was by Sweep On, whose sire, Sweep, won the Futurity and Belmont stakes among five stakes triumphs and led the sire list in 1918 and 1925. Sweep On was an adequate sire, getting eleven stakes winners.

Sweep Out had been foaled from Dugout, whose sire, Under Fire (by Swynford), sired a half-dozen stakes winners, including 1926 Kentucky Derby runner-up Bagenbaggage. Stakes-placed Dugout's dam, Cloak, was by Disguise, a son of the seminal American stallion Domino. Raced in England, Disguise defeated English Triple Crown winner Diamond Jubilee in the Jockey Club Stakes and was third behind him in the 1900 Epsom Derby. He had a nasty disposition, however, and was banished back to America by his English trainer. Disguise sired the great filly Maskette and was the broodmare sire of Man o' War's rival John P. Grier.

At the time Vanderbilt purchased Sweep Out, she was carrying the Pompey filly Outdone, who duly was foaled in the spring of 1936 and became one of the early stakes winners bred in Vanderbilt's name. Outdone won two races from twenty-one starts, earning $4,635. The high mark of her career came in the Sagamore Handicap, a Pimlico race named for her owner's farm.

The Sagamore, for two-year-olds going six furlongs, was inaugurated in 1937 at Pimlico, where Vanderbilt had purchased controlling interest and was running the show. In the first running, Vanderbilt's Pit Bull had shown the tenacity implicit in his name and won in a dead heat with Legal Light. In the second Sagamore, Outdone was nearly 18-1 but drew out to win by a length over Morstep.

Outdone was to foal three stakes winners, all by Vanderbilt's champion Discovery, who was a son of Display. The latter was by Fair Play, son of the hot-blooded Hastings. Display was a more difficult customer in terms of temperament than Nasrullah, but he, too, was a high-class winner. He took the 1926 Preakness and other stakes and earned $256,326. The dam of Discovery was Ariadne, by Light Brigade. The latter sired one of Walter Salmon's three Preakness winners, Dr. Freeland.

Discovery won twenty-seven of sixty-three races and earned $195,287. He was the champion older male two times (1935–36). His sire record of twenty-five stakes winners (8 percent) was not outstanding statistically, but as the sire of Miss Disco and Geisha, he implanted himself in history as the broodmare sire of both Bold Ruler and Native Dancer and thus into the pedigrees of a long and ongoing march of champions. Other Discovery mares included Traffic Court, dam of Hasty Road (Preakness winner) and Traffic Judge. Both Miss Disco and Traffic Court were voted Broodmare of the Year.

The three stakes-winning Discovery—Outdone siblings were the gelding Thwarted; the filly Miss Disco; and the colt Loser Weeper. Thwarted, foaled in 1943, did not win an added-money race until he was seven. That year, 1950, Thwarted won the Oaklawn and Paul Revere handicaps en route to a career record of 116 starts, thirty-two wins, and earnings of $114,920.

By the time Thwarted earned stakes status, his year-younger sister Miss Disco had scored in four stakes in 1947–48. She did not, however, achieve this for Alfred Vanderbilt.

Wartime sent Vanderbilt into battle. He was awarded the Presidential Unit Citation for his command of a PT boat in the Pacific. With such weighty issues at hand, he sold some yearlings he otherwise might have kept, and Miss Disco was among those consigned to a sale held in Meadow Brook, New York, in 1945. Sydney S. Schupper bought her for $2,100.

At two Miss Disco placed in a pair of stakes, including the Fashion, in which she was third to the year's eventual juvenile filly champion, First Flight. At three Miss Disco won the seven-furlong Test Stakes at Saratoga and finished third in the Correction Handicap. Schupper and trainer Anthony Pascuma gave her a stern assignment that year when they entered her in the Discovery Handicap. The Discovery stretched her out to one and one-eighth miles and she was facing top-class colts, including Belmont winner and champion Phalanx. Miss Disco, under 105 pounds, finished fourth behind the high-class Cosmic Bomb (126), with the previous year's champion juvenile colt, Double Jay, second and Phalanx third.

At four Miss Disco added the Interborough and American Legion handicaps to her stakes tally. Late in the year, on November 15, 1948, Miss Disco was sent out for the New Rochelle Handicap by Jake Byer, who was then training her. First run at Morris Park in 1899, the New Rochelle subsequently had been run at Belmont Park and Jamaica at various distances and by Miss Disco's era had landed at the Empire City track in Yonkers. That year the $25,000-added race was open to horses of all ages and sex categories. With a first-place prize of $19,300, it was the seventh richest among six-furlong races in the country, aside from events run only for two-year-olds. Miss Disco (112 pounds) was sixth early but challenged between horses and got up to win by a nose from the highly accomplished sprinter Buzfuz (121).

Miss Disco won again at five and six and retired with ten victories in fifty-four starts and earnings of $80,250.

A Discovery filly with sprinters' speed in high company and a degree of toughness and durability naturally came under the gaze of professional breeders such as Bull Hancock.

"I tried to buy Miss Disco several times myself," Hancock told *The Blood-Horse* in 1971, "but never made it until one day the man who owned her called me and I was able to get her for twenty-seven five ($27,500)."

At the same time, however, Hancock had missed out on a mare he was trying to purchase for Mrs.

Phipps, so he felt he should offer this patroness the opportunity to take Miss Disco. Nasrullah was by then in the picture and Hancock thought him an appropriate match. "Mrs. Phipps asked me 'What kind of family is it?' 'It's pretty good,' I said. 'She was a nice race mare and I think she'd suit Nasrullah real well.' So, she sent me a check; we bred Miss Disco to Nasrullah. So, Mrs. Phipps got Bold Ruler, and I didn't."

Around that time, Miss Disco's full brother, Loser Weeper, was adding to the family's attractiveness. The Vanderbilt homebred took a spate of high-level handicaps, nine of them in 1949 and 1950, including the Metropolitan, Suburban, Butler, and Dixie.

The transaction landing Miss Disco in Mrs. Phipps' broodmare band had transpired in time for Wheatley Stable to be the breeder of record of her first foal, Hill Rose, by Rosemont, in 1951. Mrs. Phipps took to heart the cross Hancock had suggested, and Miss Disco's next four foals were all by Nasrullah. Three of the four were stakes winners, including, of course, Bold Ruler, as well as the successful steeplechaser Independence and Nasco, who won the 1958 Saranac Handicap and placed in the Dwyer and Peter Pan handicaps.

Miss Disco was barren in 1956, then foaled a Tom Fool filly, Foolish One. Unraced Foolish One became the dam of three good stakes winners — Funny Fellow, Protanto, and Mandera. She is granddam of several others, including Touching Wood, winner of the 1982 English St. Leger.

Returned to Nasrullah, Miss Disco next foaled Eastern Princess, who placed in the Selima, Colleen, and National Stallion stakes at two and foaled the good-class stakes winner Shady Character.

Miss Disco was barren in 1959, but conceived one last time to Nasrullah in the year of his death. The resulting 1960 foal, Highness, a filly, won once in seven starts and became the second dam of several stakes winners.

Miss Disco was barren again in 1961. She was bred the next two years to Nasrullah's relative Turn-to and foaled two fillies, neither of which raced or produced anything of note. In 1965 Miss Disco produced her last foal, Great Adventure, by Nasrullah's son Nadir, a co-champion two-year-old that proved moderate at stud. Great Adventure was unraced and died at three.

By then, Miss Disco's signature foal, Bold Ruler, had become the leading stallion of his day.

CHAPTER 5

"...I seem to tread on classic ground"

—Joseph Addison

When Bold Ruler was sent by railroad to Hialeah following his juvenile campaign, questions abounded. Was this a brilliant two-year-old whose fire-works had burst and were now spent, falling into the darkness, or was this a legitimate hope for the thrills and pangs along the trail toward the Kentucky Derby, and beyond?

Whatever lay ahead, there was no doubt that he was physically a handsome fellow. By year's end, veteran observer and writer Charlie Hatton was speaking of the colt's height, 16.1 1/2 hands, as exceeding that of Nashua, and he noted that Bold Ruler was also leggier than the husky other colt. "It is about the quarters that Bold Ruler is exceptional," Hatton wrote in *Daily Racing Form*'s *American Racing Manual*. "He owns two of the straightest hind legs in training, and his hocks are far nearer the ground than most horses', affording him remarkable length from hip to hock and astonishing leverage." Fitzsimmons was quoted to the effect that Bold Ruler had the longest stride he had ever seen on a horse, but he was content to let his horseman's eye tell him this and never had the stride actually measured.

Bold Ruler was registered as a dark brown with a rough white diamond in the forehead, and in what color photography was around in that time he sometimes came off looking black, sometimes brown. He was classy and sleek, but not consistently photogenic. Many photos tend to catch an angle of head and ear that make him look vaguely mulish, while other photos interject a coarseness that was not manifest in seeing the horse in the flesh.

The artist Richard Stone Reeves, who painted Bold Ruler several times over a number of years, wrote of him: "As a 2-year-old, he gave the appearance of being tall and leggy, but as he matured he filled out and became a well-proportioned stallion but never gross or bulky. He had a very dark bay [sic] coat, almost black, and was very deep through the middle."

There is a time to stand back and gaze at a colt and a time to send him out to see whether function follows form. The time for the first test of Bold Ruler at three came on January 30, 1957. His bewildering last-place finish in the Remsen had come on November 6, 1956, so Bold Ruler had a winter layoff of less than three months before his reappearance at the races. This came at glamorous and beautiful Hialeah, a morning's drive from the Henry Carnegie Phipps home in Palm Beach.

Arcaro was plying his trade at Santa Anita and did not cross the country for the colt's three-year-old debut, so Atkinson was aboard Bold Ruler again for the seven-furlong Bahamas Stakes. Ralph Lowe's little English-bred Gallant Man had created such a good impression in winning a six-furlong allowance race and then the six-furlong Hibiscus Stakes that the Hialeah bettors made him the favorite for the Bahamas. Bold Ruler, the one-time leader of his crop, was sent off at nearly 4-1, even though he was coupled with Ogden Phipps' Bureaucracy. Those were the longest odds that had ever prevailed on Bold Ruler, and such a price was never to be had again.

Atkinson let him roll, and Bold Ruler led from the

start, even though a formidable front-runner, Federal Hill, was in the fray. A half-mile in :45 (which nearly fifty years later is still a rapid fraction) had him in front by daylight, and he drove on to get six furlongs in 1:09 1/5 and finish off in 1:22, winning by four and a half lengths. The time was a stakes record and equaled the track record set by the older Crafty Admiral under 107 pounds. The allowance conditions of the race saw Bold Ruler carrying 126 pounds and giving twelve pounds to the runner-up, Gen. Duke. The stellar eleven-horse field also included old rival King Hairan, who had won eight stakes at two when away from Bold Ruler's shadow but never regained such high status. Gallant Man might have been perceived as a flash in the pan as he finished fourth, but, in fact, trainer John Nerud would back off him for a few weeks and then produce him as a more formidable rival than might have been recognized at the time.

Two-and-a-half weeks later, Bold Ruler received a significant upgrade in assignment. This was the Everglades Stakes, which at one and one-eighth miles would be the longest race for its contenders to date and which was the final prep before the Flamingo Stakes of the same distance. Gen. Duke, who had been runner-up in the Bahamas and earlier had been beaten by Gallant Man, was back to try again. Gen. Duke was part of the Calumet Farm team, a group of three-year-olds that in 1957 was one of the strongest in the history of that long dominant stable. Although its champion two-year-old, Barbizon, never returned to top-flight form, Calumet had a rising superstar in Gen. Duke and another worthy colt in Iron Liege. Both were by the aging super stallion Bull Lea, and Iron Liege had been the star of a photographic series that *Sports Illustrated* launched at his foaling.

Gen. Duke was programmed by pedigree and preparation to improve as the months wore on and the distances stretched out. In the Everglades, he again was receiving a dozen pounds from Bold Ruler. Arcaro was back on the Wheatley Stable colt, whose Bahamas was seen to have regained at least part of his prestige, and they were favored at 2-5.

Three days before, Fitzsimmons had asked Atkinson to work Bold Ruler "a good stiff mile," and the colt had overdone it a bit by reeling off a half-mile in :45, six furlongs in 1:09 2/5, and a mile in 1:35. The Hialeah

dirt track was one and one-eighth miles in circumference and there was no mile chute; thus, one-mile races would have started on the first turn, so there was not much true value in comparing the work to the 1:36 3/5 track record Bright Willie had held since 1942. Nevertheless, it was clearly a remarkable work. The track record at Belmont Park, around one turn, was 1:34 4/5, as one illustration, while the premier one-mile event in the East, the Metropolitan Handicap, at that time had only twice been won in 1:35 and never in swifter time. Nevertheless, Fitzsimmons' public comment was "no harm done," perhaps his eighty-two-year-old sense of gentlemanly behavior reserving for private any other opinions he might have expressed to, or about, Atkinson. We doubt that Mr. Fitz spent much time walking past graveyards, but his "no harm done" comment indicates he would have known how to whistle had the occasion demanded.

On the other hand, it is possible that he was dead right and that the incredible work did not contribute to Bold Ruler's defeat in the Everglades. After all, the speed-loving colt took Arcaro on a merry run of six furlongs in 1:10 2/5 and completed a mile in 1:34 3/5, two ticks faster than the training move. At that point, the leader under 126 pounds was two lengths in front, but then was attacked and passed by the developing challenger under 114. Gen. Duke won by a head, with stablemate Iron Liege well back in third. The time of 1:47 2/5 missed the track record by only one-fifth of a second.

The late John W. Russell, who years later would train for the Phipps stable, was working for Calumet Farm's trainers, Ben and Jimmy Jones, at the time. He delighted in recalling a scene he said took place the next morning: "There were a couple trees over near the track that were close enough together for Mr. Fitz to hold onto them and do pulling exercises (straightening himself to the degree he could, given his severe slumping posture). Ben rode by and said, 'Hey. You should've been at the racetrack yesterday. They were giving money away!' "

Fitzsimmons probably just smiled and continued with his own efforts. He was not the sort we imagine quipping to Jones later: "Hey, if you're going to win one of these one and one-eighth-mile races, why not win the hundred-thousand instead of the prep?"

In fact, he would have license to say just that, for Bold Ruler took advantage of facing Gen. Duke at equal weights (122 pounds) and won the $100,000-added Flamingo Stakes when next they met.

In those days, the Flamingo Stakes had a prestige only one rung down from the Triple Crown races themselves. It was the sporting highlight of the Hialeah meeting, which, as the crème dela crème of the South Florida winter tourism season, owned a prestige and cachet even exceeding that of the similarly situated Gulfstream Park meeting of today.

The Hialeah fans did their ciphering with the equal weights and, although having seen Bold Ruler lose to Gen. Duke as a 2-5 favorite, sent the Wheatley colt back to the gate as almost as strong a choice, at 1-2. Federal Hill took off in front, leading his six rivals through a half-mile in :45 2/5. Arcaro was able to restrain Bold Ruler off the pace, something the colt would not always accept happily.

On the backstretch, Bold Ruler was three lengths off the pace of the serial speedster Federal Hill, and Gen. Duke and jockey Bill Hartack were nine lengths farther off the pace. After six furlongs in 1:10 2/5, Bold Ruler had taken a lead of one and a half lengths. Hartack attacked with Gen. Duke along an inside path left open when Dave Erb steered the lesser-light Calumet stable-mate, Iron Liege, off the rail. Nevertheless, Bold Ruler had increased his lead to two lengths at the eighth pole, having reduced his one-mile clocking again, to 1:34 2/5. Gen. Duke swung outside to charge at him again and whittled the lead to a neck, but Bold Ruler won it. The complete time of 1:47 was the fastest ever recorded by a three-year-old and took one-fifth of a second off Spartan Valor's track record set as an older horse. *American Race Horses of 1957* summarized the Flamingo as, "Gen. Duke ran a better race than in the Everglades, but so did Bold Ruler."

However, the running pattern of Gen. Duke's and Bold Ruler's swapped neck-victory races invited the thought that the free-running Bold Ruler would be in trouble when the distance stretched by an extra furlong in the Kentucky Derby. Arcaro countered this idea following the Flamingo, explaining that Bold Ruler tended to ease up after establishing a lead and asserting that, once he felt a couple of cracks of the whip, "he got to running again as soon as Gen. Duke got

alongside." Perhaps Arcaro had been past a graveyard or two himself, although, to be fair, a photo of the Flamingo finish shows him in the posture of a rider with a handful of horse, looking over his shoulder at Gen. Duke as if to make sure he was letting his own colt do just enough.

CHAPTER 6

Linking Past To Present

Despite any quibbling about stamina, the Florida campaign had verified that Wheatley Stable and Sunny Jim Fitzsimmons had a colt who justified continuation along the path to the big one, the Kentucky Derby.

For all her success, Mrs. Henry Carnegie Phipps had never won a classic, in the sense that the traditional meaning of the term "classic" is applied only to the Triple Crown races — the Derby, Preakness, and Belmont. In contrast, trainer Fitzsimmons had won classics by the dozen, all twelve for Belair Stud.

The majority of Sunny Jim's classic days had been crowded into the 1930s. He took all three Triple Crown events with Gallant Fox and his son Omaha, in 1930 and 1935, respectively. Fitzsimmons added another Derby and Belmont in 1939 with Johnstown, and had also won Belmonts with Faireno and Granville during that decade. Following a drought of sixteen years after Johnstown, he added another Preakness and Belmont Stakes with Nashua.

Such a wealth of high-class runners had become a part of Sunny Jim Fitzsimmons' life only after he neared the age of fifty. Theretofore, he had toiled in two roles — jockey and then trainer — paying his dues in a professional manner but without breaking into the top rungs of the game.

James E. Fitzsimmons was born in 1874 on Long Island in a neighborhood that five years later became the site of the Coney Island Jockey Club's handsome new Sheepshead Bay racetrack. Fitzsimmons was ten when he took his first racetrack job, doing stable and kitchen chores for the Brennan Brothers at Sheepshead Bay.

He later worked full time for the Dwyer brothers. A pair of butchers who made it big as entrepreneurs, Phil and Mike Dwyer were known for racing their horses arduously and then selling and replacing them rather than establishing a breeding operation. Fitzsimmons would likely have been introduced to what a great three-year-old is all about seventy years before Bold Ruler's classic campaign; in 1887 the Dwyers had one of their finest champions in Hanover. Winner of twenty of twenty-seven races that year, Hanover was regarded as the best horse in America. Years later, an opinion attributed to Fitzsimmons was that Miss Woodford (also owned by the Dwyers) was the greatest of American race fillies, although the lad would have been only twelve by the time of her last year of racing, in 1886.

If early days found Fitzsimmons in the association of champions, much of the next four decades was more a tale of scuffling below the top than luxuriating in racing's top rungs.

One afternoon when Fitzsimmons was about fifteen, Hardy Campbell, who had a lesser division for the Dwyers, asked the boy if he were capable of riding in a race. Butterflies notwithstanding, Fitzsimmons made his debut as a rider that afternoon, finishing fourth on a horse named Newburgh.

This was a modest launch that did not presage numerous opportunities to ride Dwyer brothers horses, what with jockeys such as future Hall of Famer Jimmy

McLaughlin on hand to guide the stable's parade of champions. Jockey Fitzsimmons headed for the lesser tracks.

Racing journalist George F.T. Ryall interviewed Fitzsimmons for a two-part article for *The Blood-Horse* in 1963, and he described Fitzsimmons' early ventures thusly: "Outlaw tracks were thicker than blackberries, and Mr. Fitz had a go at them all. 'No matter where there was racing, I was there,' he says, and he mentioned such long forgotten tracks as Maspeth on Long Island, Guttenburg and Gloucester in New Jersey, Saint Asaph and Alexander Island in Virginia, Marcus Hook, Sunny Side, and Elkton in Maryland, and Carnegie and Barksdale in Pennsylvania."

While the word "outlaw" today might be construed as meaning the lowlife of racing, it is not clear that in Fitzsimmons' day it was necessarily as pejorative a term as it seems. After all, Aqueduct, where Fitzsimmons would stable years later, was regarded as an outlaw track when it opened in 1894. At any rate, Fitzsimmons told Ryall that he had been asked to participate in some funny business in terms of winning or losing races only twice in his career.

Of course, a rider is not necessarily brought in on the deal when chicanery is afoot. One of Mr. Fitz's grandchildren, Jack Fitzsimmons, recalled his grandfather's tale of going to the post one day on a heavy favorite. The young jockey could tell by the sloshing about he heard from the horse's stomach that the animal had been filled up with water so he could not win. Having whatever stewards were around scratch the horse was not an option because Fitzsimmons needed the fee, so he carried on. The horse was well beaten and Fitzsimmons steered him to the outside rail so he could jump off and dash through the crowd before it could react to the jockey of a beaten favorite — the poor soul who would appear to be the culprit. He found the trainer and got his money.

As an old gentleman, Sunny Jim also told Jack about a track on the Maryland-Pennsylvania border. One state had blue laws against drinking on the premises, "so they just extended the bar across the state line!"

While year-round racing is sometimes seen today as the result of modern greed, both in the bosoms of tax-hungry state legislatures and within the sport itself,

Fitzsimmons' day was no different. Racing year-round in the East and Tidewater areas was a tough existence, and Fitzsimmons was a tough customer.

Well, he almost had to be. He had married at the age of seventeen and thus had responsibilities. The family story goes that his cruelly misshapen posture of later years had much to do with the practice of sweating before a brick kiln in order to keep his weight down. So urgent was the matter of putting food on the table — for his wife, if not for his weight-obsessed self — that he once sweated off eleven pounds in a day to accept the chance to earn a hundred dollars in a race. Fitzsimmons' weight-loss methods also included a homemade sweatbox and shoveling clay at a brickyard. Ryall wrote that on the occasion in question, Fitzsimmons was "pretty shaky," but he made the weight — and won the race.

The turn of the century was nearing when Fitzsimmons concluded that a turn of career path was the wise move. He bade mental farewell to whatever ambitions he might have harbored for fame and riches at the racetrack and decided to accept a steady job, with the Philadelphia street railway. A few days before this scheduled transfer of life, however, Fitzsimmons got wind of perhaps one last chance on the racetrack. A prominent Philadelphian, Colonel Edward de Veaux Morrell, was in need of a horse trainer. Fitzsimmons threw his hat into that ring and signed on with an owner who had more social prestige than those for whom he had trained in the past. (One of his owners of grist-mill type racehorses had been himself.)

Fitzsimmons was stamped with the nickname "Sunny Jim" by *New York World* sports editor George Dailey, who drew upon the name of a popular cartoon character. Fitzsimmons stayed with Morrell for about five years and was leading trainer at Maryland's Pimlico racetrack in 1904. Two years later, he launched a public stable back at Aqueduct, but this flirting with the big time did not imply a pristine milieu, for several of his owners had Tammany Hall connections.

In 1911 and 1912, racing was blacked out by anti-gambling reform, so Sunny Jim had to pack up his trappings and hit the road again. He raced in Maryland and in Canada. After New York racing was revived in 1913, the Eastern hunt clubs helped revive racing by purchasing horses in the depressed Kentucky market

and parceling them out for their members to race. Fitzsimmons spotted the opportunity to train for some socially acceptable types.

After this new leg up, he found his clientele increasing, and in 1915, Ryall wrote, Fitzsimmons won fifty-one races for the year and earned $27,890 in purses. Two years later came another change. He took the post as trainer for the Quincy Stable of James F. Johnson. Larger than most stables of the era, the Johnson string was fifty horses strong by 1920 and divided among several divisions, as is common today.

After years of outlaw tracks and Tammany Hall owners, Fitzsimmons perhaps had license to think that not only the straight and narrow, but also the visibility of pursuing that path lay before him. Then, controversy reared its head, and it put Quincy Stable in conflict with one of the richest and most important owners of the day, Harry Sinclair of Rancocas Stable.

Johnson had made an astute purchase, Playfellow, a full brother to the heroic Man o' War. In 1921, the year after Man o' War's retirement, Playfellow came to hand and won a couple of races with high style. Given the enormous prestige and worldwide fame of the colt's full brother, this was enough to bring Sinclair to the Quincy Stable, and he paid $100,000 for Playfellow.

Alas, the younger brother to greatness lost his next two races and Sinclair was unhappy with him, and the deal. He claimed that the colt was a cribber, and he sued the previous owner to right the perceived wrong. The trial ended in a deadlock, although Fitzsimmons and Johnson had the seemingly sound defense that the horse had surely exhibited no debilitating windsucking traits at the time he won the two races that attracted Sinclair to him in the first place! Johnson grew discouraged about even being in the horsc game.

In his late forties, Sunny Jim Fitzsimmons was adrift again. Then, in 1923, his path coincided with that of one William Woodward Sr., a fellow of distinguished banking heritage and a sporting inclination that would gather distinction for the remaining three decades of his life. Fitzsimmons was offered the job of training Woodward's nascent stable — to be renowned as Belair Stable. Shakespeare's "tide in the affairs of man" at last had swept up to the hardworking and already physically bent Sunny Jim Fitzsimmons, and

he had the savvy to take it “at the flood” which “leads on to fortune.”

Champion Thoroughbreds awaited, and Fitzsimmons knew just what to do when they came his way.

Four decades of major stakes winners followed, horses such as the Triple Crown winners Gallant Fox and Omaha, the Horse of the Year Nashua, champion fillies High Voltage and Misty Morn, and then Bold Ruler and his early crops of stakes winners. Fitzsimmons did not retire until 1963. About a dozen years earlier, he had lost his wife, Jennie Harvey Fitzsimmons, that girl who plighted her troth with a teenager so many years before and who had helped him make life work — whatever it took. If there was a weak spine in the family in the medical sense, there surely had been nothing but the strongest of backbones in human character and resilience. Mr. Fitz passed away in 1966.

The couple had six children and seventeen grandchildren. One of the grandchildren, the New York-based equine veterinarian Bob Carr, verified a quip once attributed to Mr. Fitz, i.e., that he had so much trouble remembering the grandchildren’s names that their mothers were somewhat put off.

"He would tend to call me and my two brothers Carr-y, at least recognizing what family I was in," Bob Carr told the author. "I am sure my cousins all had similar experience. My mother was his daughter Edyth. Just about all the various Fitzsimmons family grew up in Brooklyn. My grandfather and several of the sons' families grew up in the Sheepshead Bay section. I grew up in the Marine Park (Flatbush) section, about ten minutes from Sheepshead Bay."

Carr recalled that Mr. Fitz had an aversion to seeing any of the grandchildren gravitate to the racetrack. Carr persevered and, once his grandfather was convinced that the young man was determined to see through his ambition to become a veterinarian — with or without the old man's help — young Carr was allowed to work for Mr. Fitz as a groom, but only for a summer (1958) and after "he was quite sure I was attending college at Cornell." (Carr graduated in 1963, the year Mr. Fitz retired.)

Jack Fitzsimmons, seventy-two in 2005, recalled that his grandfather's aversion to seeing the next generation get involved was because the racetrack routine

and long hours seven days a week are tough on family life. Jack Fitzsimmons' father, John, was the oldest of the Fitzsimmons' children.

"He was a very good artist. He went to art school," Jack Fitzsimmons said of his own father. "But in these Irish families, the oldest son has to help the father. So he gave that up and went to work for his father. After my grandfather retired, my father went back to art and did a lot of paintings of horses. My father was the stable manager, and two of my uncles, Jim and Harvey, were assistant trainers."

Despite Sunny Jim Fitzsimmons' feeling about the grandchildren and racing, it was a family affair around his barn. One of Sunny Jim's brothers, Tom, was a long-time assistant and, in addition to sons John, Jim, and Harvey, several other relatives and in-laws had jobs connected to the racetrack, frontside or backside. Grandson Jack never worked for his father but had many jobs as mutuel clerk, fence painter, elevator operator, and gate crew assistant from Longacres to Saratoga as he worked through Notre Dame, served in the Army, and attended law school. Horses were in his blood, too, and while working as an attorney in

Maryland he for many years would train a few horses on a training track near his home and race them at area tracks.

As for the younger generation's interaction with their famous grandfather in his work place, Carr said, "I can best describe us as 'special interest spectators.' We had many wonderful, exciting days — birthday parties and such — at the track, but it was always a social venture and he truly enjoyed such gatherings. He simply did not discuss any of the day-to-day happenings at the barn, certainly not with me ... His excitement level never seemed to change — by the time I was old enough to be aware, anyway. He had long since made his mark and his job was never in jeopardy. The nearest I can recall his being especially attentive was the match race (Belair's Nashua vs. Swaps in 1955). He definitely wanted to win that badly and, of course, did."

Carr described his grandfather's disfigurement as eventually being "nearly a 90 degree position all the time. He had difficulty standing and speaking with people and preferred to sit so he could speak face to face. He had a wonderful sense of humor, and I never

heard him complain about his back. I assume it had become so chronic that the pain level was very minimal, if (there was pain) at all."

CHAPTER 7

Appellation Spring

A half-dozen years before his retirement, Fitzsimmons was swept up in the campaign of one more potential champion. Bold Ruler and Gen. Duke tarried in Florida for an additional epic meeting after the Flamingo. This would come four weeks later, on March 30, in the Florida Derby at Gulfstream Park, another $100,000 classic prep at one and one-eighth miles. Although Bold Ruler had that sprint win over Gen. Duke in the Bahamas, the Florida Derby was essentially a "rubber match" after their alternating wins at nine furlongs.

The brilliance of the top pair discouraged assembly of a large field, and the Florida Derby post parade was an affair of only five entrants. Under the allowance conditions of the race, Bold Ruler, Gen. Duke, and Federal Hill carried 122 pounds while Iron Liege and

Shan Pac got in with 118. Bold Ruler was 3-5. The minutely more liberal odds than in the Flamingo presumably reflected the impression Gen. Duke had made in winning the Fountain of Youth in the interim, plus the fact that he again had his stablemate, Iron Liege, coupled with him in the betting.

To quote *American Race Horses of 1957*, "the hindsight of one race is foresight to another, but not necessarily the foresight that leads to success." By that volume's interpretation, Arcaro had concluded from the Flamingo that Bold Ruler was best ridden when restrained off the pace. And, of course, with Federal Hill in any race, the wiser part of valor generally equated with avoiding a duel on the front end. Grand Prix auto racing of the era had two superstars, Stirling Moss and Juan Fangio. Moss lived by the credo of going as fast as you could as far as you could, and he was often on the sidelines before the finish, whereas the controlled Fangio frequently came along to win without abusing his car. Federal Hill and Stirling Moss were kindred spirits.

Arcaro held Bold Ruler off the pace as Federal Hill took the Florida Derby field through swift, but not outlandish, fractions, getting five furlongs in :58 2/5 and six furlongs in 1:10 2/5. Aside from Shan Pac, the rest of the field was in a bunch as they raced by the furlong pole, Bold Ruler a head in front with another of his prodigious one-mile clockings, this one in 1:34 3/5. Nevertheless, Gen. Duke had the greater momentum, and he sailed past, winning by one and a half lengths. Bold Ruler had only a head margin for second over Iron Liege. Federal Hill finished last but was beaten only five lengths.

All winter and spring the Eastern three-year-olds had hung up eye-catching times, and on this occasion Gen. Duke bettered Bold Ruler's gaudy Flamingo clocking by one-fifth of a second. The fastest time on record for a three-year-old had survived only four weeks, and Gen. Duke's 1:46 4/5 not only usurped that distinction but also matched the prevailing world record.

A few weeks later the articulate and outspoken Arcaro gave a detailed commentary of the Flamingo and Florida Derby to the *New York Times'* Arthur Daley:

"In the Flamingo, Gen. Duke moved to me on the stretch turn. I was watching him and when he came to me I set my horse down and we drew away and I

thought we were holding him at the finish. I think Gen. Duke was closer to me twenty yards up the track than he was at the wire, and I felt like my horse was ready to draw away from him at the finish.

"In the Florida Derby, Gen. Duke made me move sooner, going into the turn. He wasn't more than a neck off me ... and when he dropped back a length and a half I thought I had killed him off in that eighth of a mile. When the other Calumet, Iron Liege, moved on the rail turning for home, he was behind Federal Hill and I wasn't worried because I had him safe in a pocket there on the inside. In the stretch, Federal Hill came off the rail and Iron Liege got through, got a neck ahead of me at one point, and although I don't hit this horse (Bold Ruler) much I gave him a couple of belts to beat Iron Liege for second money. Gen. Duke, coming again on the outside, had no trouble beating us.

"Afterward, Willie Hartack said he took Gen. Duke back off me to give the horse a breather, but I looked at the movies and I don't believe it. If I'm in contention and he's got me by the head at the five-sixteenths pole, he's not so generous that he'll spot me a length and a half from there. What I think is his horse was floundering and Willie is a sharp boy and he had the sense to gather his horse and steady him down before moving again. I don't think Bold Ruler was on his 'A' game that day."

Bold Ruler was clearly a very brilliant horse, but thoughts of Calumet's nonpareil racehorse, Triple Crown winner Citation, had begun to creep into the mindset of those who contemplated Gen. Duke!

The Wheatley team licked its wounds and headed back up north, but Fitzsimmons kept Bold Ruler on the Derby trail.

Bold Ruler was the 1-2 choice in a seven-horse field for the Wood Memorial, in which all carried their Derby weight of 126 pounds. John Nerud had freshened Gallant Man, who was 8-1 at post time, and the trainer was about to show the world that he had more or less reinvented the speedster from the Florida winter.

Bold Ruler established the lead early with exemplary consistency of pace, getting quarter-miles in :24 each. After fractions of :24, :48, and 1:12, he was challenged by Gallant Man, and as they battled through the final turn the other colt got the lead. Jockey Johnny Chouquette was not a headliner, but he had

gotten a taste of the big time as the rider of champion Needles in several of that colt's summer juvenile stakes wins two years earlier, and the jockey was hell-bent to get the job done on Nerud's suddenly potent Derby candidate.

They hit the mile mark in 1:36 1/5, seemingly unimpressive after the winter of rapid miles, but Jamaica's odd, sort of egg-shaped circuit made the time deceptive. Gallant Man held sway by a small margin through most of the final furlong, but with Arcaro whipping away on his left side, Bold Ruler surged enough to get the win by a nose. The time of 1:48 4/5 was not impressive if compared to the Florida records, but it was the fastest ever recorded for nine furlongs at the unique Jamaica track.

Columnist Daley recorded an enthusiastic byplay between winning and losing jockey, who still seemingly had a bit of adrenaline churning.

Chouquette: "I'll tell you this. We'd have won if my horse ever had run a distance race in his whole life. He'd never run this far before. I really thought I had you at the sixteenth pole."

Arcaro: "Mine is a game dude. When your horse

had a neck on him, mine didn't stop."

Chouquette: "Mine is a short-necked horse. That big colt of yours runs with his neck stretched out. Maybe that explains it." (Daley noted that the beaten rider was "groping," but of course he had no notion of what a length of neck might foretell for the next race.)

Arcaro: "When you went by me, I had to get my horse to run again. I don't like to hit this colt because it usually don't do any good. But I had to do something. You were so close alongside me that I couldn't hit him right-handed. So I busted him lefty."

Arcaro concluded by comparing Bold Ruler with a former mount: "He's easier to ride than Nashua, but I still don't know if he's a better horse."

The Kentucky Derby came up two weeks later, on May 4. For a stable headquartered in New York and steeped in the traditions of the great New York races, the Derby was important but perhaps not seen as the Holy Grail to the extent other echelons regarded it. Mrs. Phipps' son Ogden once said that the Belmont Stakes for years had been the ultimate target — while noting that one took care in just what company such observations could be expressed — but the Derby cer-

tainly, over the years, had grown in stature as a revered goal. His mother's Wheatley Stable had a Derby record that indicated a recognition of the importance of the Louisville race. Wheatley had been thirteenth with one of those early purchases, Distraction, in 1928, eighth with Teufel in 1936, and fourth with Melodist in 1937. All three had won the Wood Memorial, and now Bold Ruler had won it, too, and he was on his way to Louisville.

From 1930 through 1942, Sunny Jim Fitzsimmons had run nine horses in seven Derbys and had won three. (In 1936 he entered not only Teufel for Wheatley, but also Merry Pete and Granville for Belair Stud. This pre-Wayne Lukas-era numbers team produced dismal results: Granville dropped his rider soon after the start; Merry Pete finished tenth and Teufel, eighth.) In 1955, when he had the favorite in Nashua, Fitzsimmons declined the trip, given the difficulties of travel in his octogenarian status. Grandson Jack Fitzsimmons recalled that his father, John, went to Louisville to represent Mr. Fitz at various social events and that his Uncle Jim, an assistant trainer in the hands-on horsemanship sense, also went. He assumed that the younger Jim Fitzsimmons saddled Nashua, who was upset by Swaps.

Jack Fitzsimmons recalled that his grandfather's decision to attend Bold Ruler's Derby had more to do with how the old man was feeling at the time than the fact that Nashua had been beaten in his absence.

What a Derby the 1957 running shaped up to be. A writer as savvy as Tower knew that tossing around the word "great" about three-year-olds in the spring was more hyperbole than horse wisdom. After all, he was Harry Payne Whitney's grandson! Yet, the consistency of eye-catching performances from the classic contenders of 1957 convinced horsemen as well as fans that it was, potentially, at least, an exceptional crop.

For Tower's last pre-Derby piece in *Sports Illustrated,* the headline writer extolled "A Year of Greatness." This was not exaggeration, or taking license. Probably harking back mentally to his year-old comments about Bold Ruler, et al., Tower began his lead thusly:

"To talk so soon of 'greatness' in connection with the current crop of 3-year-old Thoroughbreds would normally be singularly audacious. For this [the word "great"] is an accolade not lightly awarded by horse-

men. [One can only wonder whether this can be said of many of today's horsemen and fans, conditioned by modern, minimalist campaigns.]

"One sensational race should never qualify its winner as great. [But] there has not been one sensational race in 1957. There have been at least a half-dozen."

Tower understood that a fast time here and there can be more a function of pace, track condition, etc., than a true definition of quality. In the winter-spring of 1957, though, it was not a matter of a bright spot here and there, but a pattern of record-equaling and record-setting times that created an aura of excellence from not one but a series of horses.

As described above, Bold Ruler and Gen. Duke had gone record-tie, record-set, or world-record tie in race after race. Federal Hill — an enabler of good clockings via his own prodigious early speed — had equaled the nine-furlong record at Fair Grounds in winning the Louisiana Derby when for once he could duck the Bold Ruler-Gen. Duke cartel. Iron Liege turned the tables on Gen. Duke in an allowance prep at Keeneland and did it in track-record time for seven furlongs, and Round Table seemed to be peaking at just the right moment when he set the track record at Keeneland while winning the one and one-eighth-mile Blue Grass Stakes.

Round Table was late in implanting himself into this aura of brilliance at three, although he had been a quick study at two. He was bred by A.B. Hancock Jr. and was foaled at Claiborne Farm on the same night — April 6, 1954 — as Bold Ruler. He carried the Claiborne silks to stakes triumphs at two, then was sold for a price generally reported at $145,000 to Oklahoma oilman Travis Kerr during the winter of 1957.

Jimmy Jones, trainer of Gen. Duke, Iron Liege, and the struggling Barbizon, spoke at a dinner at Keeneland, where his father was being honored, and addressed the prevailing opinion about the exceptional three-year-olds of the season:

"From a spectator's standpoint, I don't think there has ever been anything like it before."

As matters turned out, on Derby Eve, Jones announced that, although Gen. Duke was entered, he doubted that his big star and probable favorite could actually start. The horse had a nagging hoof bruise. Later, Gen. Duke was indeed scratched. (In a hopeful moment Jones sent Gen. Duke to Pimlico to train for

the Preakness, but eventually the "bruise" was found to be a fracture of a pedal bone. In a stunning downward spiral of life's fortunes, Gen. Duke never raced again and, diagnosed as a wobbler, was humanely destroyed without even the opportunity to stand at stud.)

The quality of the expected contenders had the effect of reducing the numbers for the Kentucky Derby. The field of nine that walked into the decibels of "My Old Kentucky Home" on May 4, 1957, constituted the smallest gathering for the Derby since Calumet's Citation-Coaltown entry had frightened off all but four adventurers in 1948.

Bold Ruler was the 6-5 choice, as Arcaro sought to add to his record number of five Derby wins. Round Table was second choice at 3.60-1 and Gallant Man next at 3.70-1. Federal Hill, although he could have been cast as the "Speed Kills" poster child, was owned by Louisville's Clifford Lussky and had won the Derby Trial, so he was fairly well backed at 7.90-1. Iron Liege, who all winter had been consistently beaten by the best but consistently remained a contender, had finished next to last in the Derby Trial on Tuesday and was relegated to 8.40-1 as the seemingly forlorn survivor of the once-brazen Calumet brigade.

As will happen now and again in a horse race, surprises awaited.

Federal Hill charged into the lead, and Arcaro, feeling he had nothing to fear from that one, especially going one and a quarter miles, sought to restrain Bold Ruler. The colt who had allowed him to do this in the Flamingo wanted to go on with the pace on Derby Day and fought the waiting tactic. Federal Hill raced a quarter-mile in :23 3/5, a half-mile in :47, and six furlongs in 1:11 2/5. By that time, it was Iron Liege who had snuck up to be second, a half-length off the lead, while Bold Ruler was one and a half lengths farther back. Turning for home, Federal Hill clung to the last vestiges of his lead. The mile was run in 1:36 4/5 and then Iron Liege took over. Arcaro could not get Bold Ruler to keep pace, but Bill Shoemaker was charging up on Gallant Man. Through the stretch Gallant Man was gradually getting to Iron Liege, it seemed, and then Shoemaker mistook the sixteenth pole for the finish and raised in his irons for a millisecond. It was probably the most famous miscue by a jockey in Derby history. Fortunately, for Shoemaker, however, his status was already so entrenched that he could withstand it and go on to so successful a career that for some thirty years he held the all-time record for number of wins.

Iron Liege, the weak half of the anticipated Calumet entry, held on to win by a nose in 2:02 1/5. The crop that had set or matched numerous records produced a Derby four-fifths of a second over Whirlaway's record. The time was slower than four of the last seven runnings.

For Calumet Farm, winning the classic for the sixth time, such details were not of overriding importance. If *Sports Illustrated* were destined to be known for its "cover jinx," the magazine surely did no mischief to the chances of a foal it had depicted in the first wet moments of life back in 1954.

Round Table finished third, nearly three lengths behind runner-up Gallant Man, and he had three lengths on the disappointing Bold Ruler. Wheatley, Wood Memorial, Kentucky Derby: They were not a charmed trio.

Shoemaker manfully admitted to the most glaring mistake of the 1957 Kentucky Derby, but Arcaro came around to the thought that he had made perhaps a more significant miscalculation. By the end of the next week, he was detailing for columnist Red Smith his own culpability. Arcaro concluded he had simply fought the colt too much too early.

"You see, before the Derby Mr. Fitz and I felt the main one we had to beat was Gallant Man," Arcaro told Smith.

"We felt we could take Federal Hill any time we wanted to, and we weren't too much afraid of Iron Liege because we had always beaten him. So, it seemed to us it would be foolish to use up Bold Ruler running with Federal Hill and let Gallant Man come on at the end to nail both of us. Mr. Fitz told me, 'Take back off Federal Hill a little, let him go out on the lead if he wants to.'

"That's what I was trying to do on the first run past the stands, but Bold Ruler went into the clubhouse turn like a wild horse. He was so full of run he could have gone right on past Federal Hill and I should have let him do that, but it wasn't until then that I realized I was fighting him too hard. By then it was too late."

In 2005 it would be stupefying to ask a trainer if he were planning to run a disappointing Derby favorite between then and the Preakness. In 1957, though, that

was exactly what Sunny Jim Fitzsimmons did. The fact that on the Saturday between the two classics Pimlico carded a race named the Preakness Prep underscores the difference in approach nearly fifty years ago. Bold Ruler won the one and one-sixteenth-mile Preakness Prep, but he did it in a way that would have made Nasrullah and Nashua snicker had they been creatures who could grasp nuance.

Fitzsimmons equipped Bold Ruler with blinkers for the Preakness Prep, but they were not particularly effective. The horse had only two opponents in an event that appeared so non-competitive that the track ran it as a betless exhibition. A maiden, Convoy, outran Bold Ruler early, and Arcaro had to put his charge under the whip to convince him ultimately to win by a length over Inswept. The time of 1:43 3/5 was acceptable but not memorable.

Fitzsimmons determined to leave the blinkers on for the Preakness, and they stayed standard equipment. The blinkers were half-cups with a slit cut in the back to give the colt some back vision. Moreover, Fitzsimmons had concluded that the sensitivity of Bold Ruler's mouth, dating from that damaged tongue incident, might account for his resentment at being restrained. Fitzsimmons came up with what in the Army would be called a "field expedient." He cut off a piece of leg bandage, rolled it with cotton into a soft string, and tied it onto the bridle in such a way that the bit put more pressure on the jaw and less on the mouth.

(There was quite a run on ideas about adding equipment to Bold Ruler's headpiece. One of Fitzsimmons' granddaughters, John's daughter Kathleen, had arranged for Bold Ruler's bridle to be adorned with a religious medal she had brought back from Rome, festooned with some ribbon from Nashua's 1955 Preakness triumph. Moreover, retired police officer John Byrne, a sort of bodyguard for the fragile Mr. Fitz, was overheard by reporter Tower to say he had placed another medal on the other side of the bridle. Bold Ruler was destined to carry a lot of weight later in an official sense. This was a different matter.)

The second leg of the Triple Crown had only a seven-horse field, and Iron Liege was the only one Arcaro figured was a real danger unless something went awry again. Round Table had gone back to his West Coast base, where after a loss against older hors-

Bold Ruler proved his brilliance both on the racetrack (below at Pimlico with Eddie Arcaro and groom Robert C. Bittrolff) and in the stud (right, as a stallion at Claiborne Farm).

Bold Ruler received speed and class from his sire, Nasrullah (above left), and grandsire, Nearco (top), and toughness and heart from his dam, Miss Disco (left), and her sire, Discovery (below).

Bold Ruler was bred and owned by Mrs. Gladys Phipps (right and below, leading Bold Ruler to the winner's circle), who raced in the name of Wheatley Stable. Bold Ruler's regular rider was the Master himself, Eddie Arcaro.

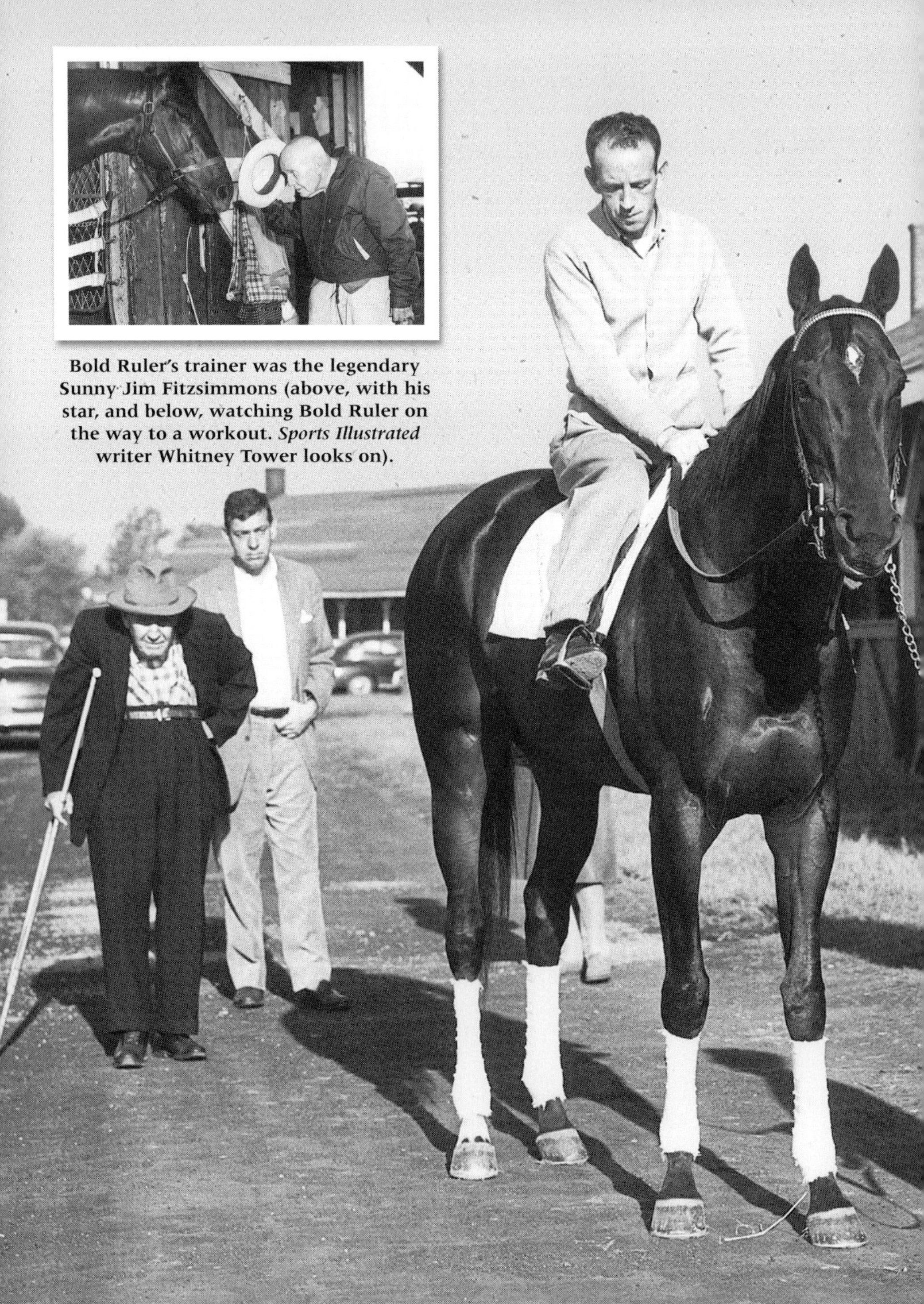

Bold Ruler's trainer was the legendary Sunny Jim Fitzsimmons (above, with his star, and below, watching Bold Ruler on the way to a workout. *Sports Illustrated* writer Whitney Tower looks on).

Ted Atkinson rode Bold Ruler to victory in the Youthful Stakes (right) for the colt's first stakes win. Arcaro was up for Bold Ruler's next stakes victory, the Juvenile on Belmont's straight Widener Chute (below). The colt later added a Futurity win (bottom).

At three, Bold Ruler alternated wins in the Bahamas (below) and Flamingo (right) at Hialeah with seconds to Gen. Duke in the Everglades and Florida Derby. In New York, Bold Ruler captured the Wood Memorial (below right) by a nose in his final Kentucky Derby prep.

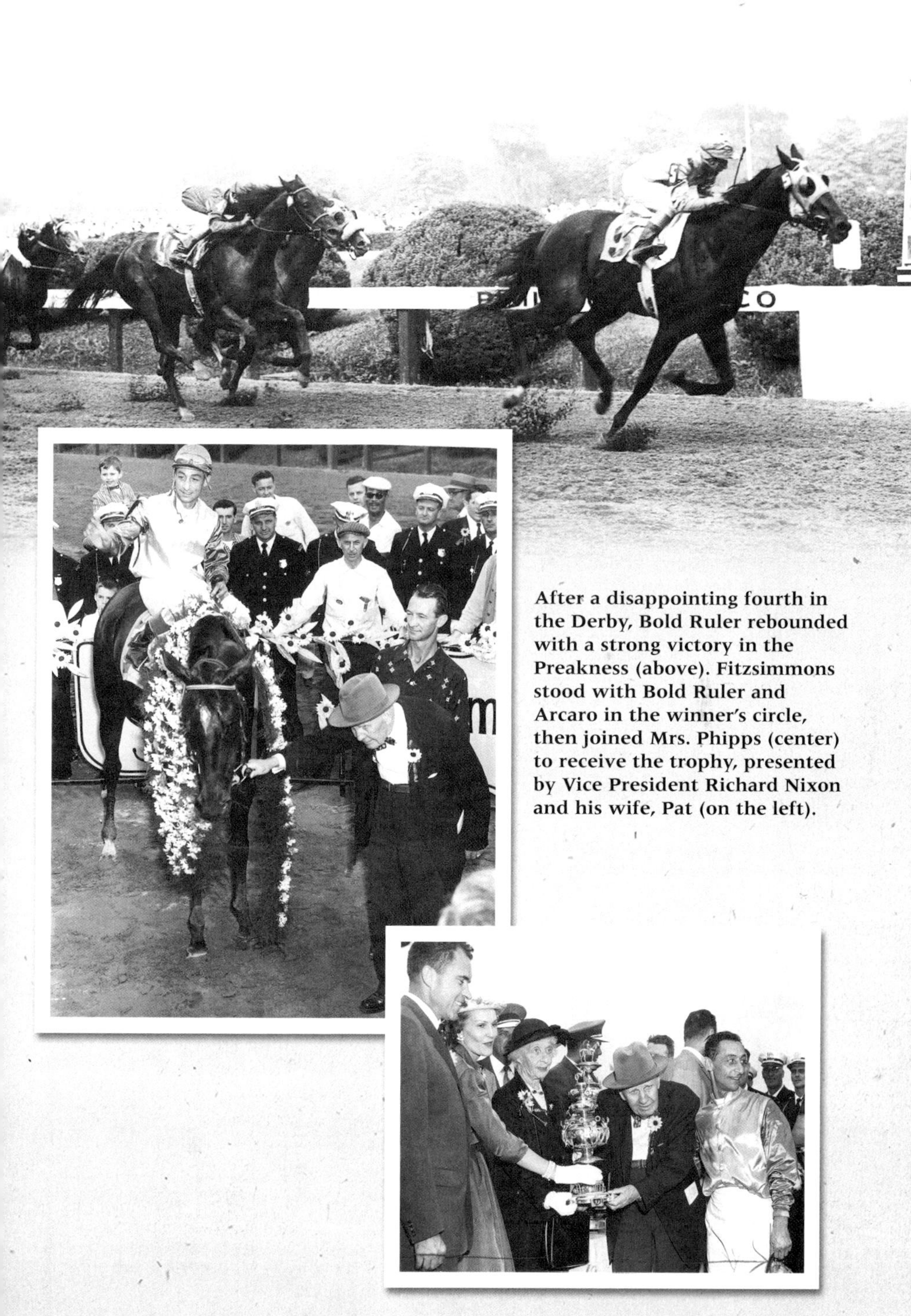

After a disappointing fourth in the Derby, Bold Ruler rebounded with a strong victory in the Preakness (above). Fitzsimmons stood with Bold Ruler and Arcaro in the winner's circle, then joined Mrs. Phipps (center) to receive the trophy, presented by Vice President Richard Nixon and his wife, Pat (on the left).

After a third to Gallant Man in the Belmont, Bold Ruler easily won an overnight handicap there (right). He carried 130 pounds for the first time in winning the Jerome Handicap (above). Later that year he charged through the slop to take the Benjamin Franklin Handicap at Garden State under 136 pounds (below).

Bold Ruler's victory over Gallant Man and Round Table in the Trenton Handicap (right) clenched Horse of the Year honors for the Wheatley runner (above in November 1957). Working to return at four (top, with Arcaro aboard), Bold Ruler didn't make his seasonal bow until May 1958 because of nagging problems.

The Wheatley champion returned victorious at four in the Toboggan Handicap (top), then quickly added the Carter (right). He carried 133 pounds and 135 pounds, respectively.

After finishing second to Gallant Man in the Met Mile, Bold Ruler led from start to finish under 133 pounds to win the Stymie Handicap by five lengths (above and below).

In the Suburban (below), Bold Ruler (on inside) just edged a stubborn Clem by a nose. The Monmouth Handicap was a little easier, Bold Ruler winning by three-quarters of a length. Fitzsimmons and Mrs. Phipps joined Bold Ruler in the Monmouth winner's circle (above).

After an injury forced his retirement, Bold Ruler was sent to A.B. Hancock Jr.'s Claiborne Farm in Kentucky for stud duty, and the horse became an instant stallion success.

Bold Ruler died on July 12, 1971, after undergoing treatment for cancer. He had already led the general sire list a record seven times but added to his glory the year after his death by leading the list for an eighth time.

es he launched an eleven-race winning streak. Gallant Man went back to New York to aim for the Belmont Stakes.

Arcaro and Fitzsimmons figured Federal Hill would again charge to the lead and Bill Hartack would have Iron Liege stalking him. The rest of the field figured to lay back and hope they could close late in the game. "So, where does that leave me and Bold Ruler?" Arcaro mused to the press. "It means I either try and rate him off Federal Hill — which is how I got him beat in the Derby — or I run with him into the first turn and keep Federal Hill on my outside at all times. Ordinarily, I hate to go running after any sprinter, but Mr. Fitz and I talked the whole thing over and we both agree that the only thing I do this time is to run for it all the way and make the horses come get you."

Tower summarized some of the public's conjecture over Bold Ruler's failure in the Derby: "Some said he had had too much racing. Some said his back was hurting him again. Some said he was overrated to begin with. And many others simply shrugged and said, in effect, 'what can you expect from a Nasrullah, anyway?' "

Bold Ruler certainly had soundness problems from time to time. For the Preakness trainer Fitzsimmons took the precaution of having exercise rider Tommy Quinn warm him up prior to the race by riding the colt from the stable area to the saddling paddock. "I want him to get limbered up," Mr. Fitz said. "I don't do this often, but I want to do it today." As we shall see, there was also at least one thread of evidence that the Preakness was the first race in which Bold Ruler benefited from the relief of soreness provided by a new medication on the scene, Butazolidin.

Iron Liege was a slight favorite, 1.30-1 to the 1.40-1 odds on Bold Ruler. Arcaro and Bold Ruler dictated their preferred scenario, aside from the colt still being a bit rank in the early going. Bold Ruler scudded to the lead early, held the rail, and raced head and head with Federal Hill. After six furlongs in 1:10 3/5, Bold Ruler had a length lead and Iron Liege had already displaced Federal Hill in second.

Hartack waited another sixteenth of a mile, until the three-eighths pole, to ask Iron Liege to fire, but even his best effort made no impression on Bold Ruler. The Wheatley colt swept around the turn with a one and a

half-length lead after a mile in 1:36 3/5. Hartack later lamented: "I had a clear shot at him, but when I asked my horse to move he had nothing to give me ... I felt at all times in this race that Bold Ruler had me over a barrel and there was nothing I could do about it."

Bold Ruler carried on, drawing out to a two-length margin at about the eighth pole and holding that same edge at the finish. The nine-furlong clocking was 1:49 and the final time was 1:56 1/5. In matters of pure speed, Bold Ruler's career image generally saw him as the more impressive in the inevitable comparison to Nashua, but in this case the final clocking was one and three-fifths seconds slower than the Preakness record Nashua had hung up two years earlier.

Mrs. Henry Carnegie Phipps had her first classic winner. Sunny Jim Fitzsimmons had his thirteenth. (This mark stood alone as the record for the remainder of the century, and then D. Wayne Lukas matched it, with Commendable in the 2000 Belmont Stakes.) Vice President Richard Nixon was on hand to fete the victors in the 1957 Preakness winner's circle.

The roller coaster winter-spring now had one more thrill ahead, the one and a half miles of the Belmont

Stakes, back at Wheatley's spiritual base, New York.

Bold Ruler thrived in the month that then lay between the Preakness and the Belmont Stakes. During the week of the big race, he worked a mile in 1:38, and Arcaro came back saying, "He never felt like this before. He was strong, willing, kept his mind on his work, did everything I asked."

Only six horses were entered for the Belmont Stakes, and the guaranteed fast-pace scenario that Federal Hill had scripted into virtually all of Bold Ruler's recent races was now dependent on a newcomer to the scene. Federal Hill had come out of his last-place Preakness finish with a touch of lameness that ended his campaign, and his handlers quite likely would have skipped the Belmont in any case.

Bold Ruler's free-running strategy in the Preakness had seemed to solve one problem, but it had created another in that it revealed to his rivals a way to bring him down. Run fast enough long enough and Bold Ruler (a/k/a Stirling Moss) would bring about his own exhaustion. Gallant Man's trainer, John Nerud, was among those who saw the obvious, so he dealt himself an extra card.

Ironically, when Ralph Lowe bought a draft of young horses from the Aga Khan, Gallant Man had been looked upon as the weak one of the litter, while a full brother to the champion Tulyar was the prized pick. As their racing careers unfolded, however, it was Gallant Man starring and the other colt, Bold Nero, toiling in oblivion. Bold Nero had enough speed to be a pest, however, and he was sent out to be the sacrificial pacemaker.

Bettors put their faith in Bold Ruler, but only by a slight margin, as they pondered his adeptness at one and a half miles. Both he and the Lowe entry were odds-on, the Wheatley colt at 17-20, the other pair at 19-20. Gallant Man, with Shoemaker forgiven by Lowe and Nerud, had warmed up by winning the Peter Pan Handicap.

Bold Ruler set out in front, and the other "Bold" went with him, prompting him through early fractions swifter than those[1] that been praised after the considerably shorter Wood Memorial. Bold Ruler sailed along in :23 2/5, :23 2/5, and :23 3/5 — 1:10 2/5 for six furlongs. Bold Nero was beginning to fade and eventually was pulled up, but he had burned out Bold Ruler's chance. Bold Ruler slowed to :25 1/5 for the next quarter-mile but had pulled away to a three-length lead. At that point he had run a mile in 1:35 3/5, and he still had a half-mile to run!

Shoemaker had bided his time on Gallant Man, in fourth place early, before advancing to second after a mile. Bold Ruler toiled on, getting the next quarter-mile in another :25 4/5, at which point he had run the Derby distance in 2:01 2/5. (Whirlaway held the Derby record in the identical time.) He clung to a head lead at the quarter-mile pole but was easily picked off by Gallant Man's smooth stamina. The little Lowe runner was in front by daylight by the eighth pole, and the only questions were how far would he win by and would Bold Ruler hold on for second? The answer to the first question was "eight lengths," and the answer to the second was "no." Inside Tract, who later developed into a Jockey Club Gold Cup (two miles) winner, stayed on well enough to pass the exhausted favorite and beat him by four lengths.

With the rapid pace and his staying power, Gallant Man set an American record as well as a track and stakes standard. His 2:26 3/5 was a second faster than

the fifteen-year-old track mark set by the excellent stayer Bolingbroke. It was one and three-fifths seconds faster than the previous Belmont Stakes record shared by a pair of great colts and Triple Crown winners — Count Fleet and Citation.

The long journey of the Triple Crown was over, and the races had yielded three different winners. Often, this is seen as indication of an indifferent crop, but while it might have given pause to the acclamations of greatness on the 1957 three-year-old scene, more brilliance lay ahead.

CHAPTER 8

"...champions fierce strive for mastery"

—John Milton

For most Thoroughbreds, maintaining a record of "win a few, lose a lot" is a pretty admirable achievement. For a horse as good as Bold Ruler, though, the swings of fortune to this point in his career had seemed more dramatic than would be anticipated. To summarize: Bred in the purple, but with a lingering hernia problem as a foal; brilliant early on at two, but stopped by an injury; an apparent champion in early autumn, but dismal in two straight races; brilliant comeback, great speed, but left Florida clearly second-best; great approach to the Kentucky Derby, but unplaced; won Preakness, scuttled in Belmont.

If those patterns might leave one dizzy, the next two months introduced new dramas, which were as mysterious as they were worrisome. Following the Belmont Stakes, Bold Ruler was not put on any intended long layoff. He was being pointed for the Arlington Classic in Chicago, which came up a month after the Triple Crown concluded. This trip was cancelled, though, when the colt appeared distressed following a workout.

"He took an awful long time cooling out after that work," Fitzsimmons said following Bold Ruler's six-furlong spin. "Just what the situation is with him, I don't know. I do know that it isn't a splint [which had surfaced after the Belmont but had responded to treatment]."

In August, Bold Ruler's condition was a topic at The Jockey Club Round Table in Saratoga, an event generally meant to address the larger issues facing the sport rather than a single colt. At that time, as reported by Bob Horwood in the *Morning Telegraph* (then the Eastern sister publication of *Daily Racing Form*), Dr. William O. Reed had described his decision to administer an encephalitis shot to Bold Ruler as being based on his diagnosis that the colt had a "heart condition."

At about the same time, on August 14, a young writer, Bill Leggett, who, along with Whitney Tower, was supplying racing news to *Sports Illustrated* in those days, filed a lengthy piece that included the following comment about Bold Ruler attributed to Mr. Fitz:

"He won't be racing until the fall. It's a peculiar thing about him. He can gallop five miles and it won't hurt him, but if I breeze him five furlongs he comes back to his stall a little lame. I keep him in Stall 49, right at the very end of the barn. I've kept all my good horses there — Gallant Fox, Omaha, Granville, Nashua. There have been a lot of good horses in that stall. He's a good one, too. The real trouble with him is that his right shoulder muscle hurts him; it hurts him especially when he exerts himself. We have been rubbing it with liniment and using a microtherm machine. It's sort of like arthritis, but he'll be all right. It will just take time."

Earlier, around Belmont Stakes time, Red Smith's column had included a most mysterious quote from Fitzsimmons. According to Smith, Mr. Fitz revealed the following:

"He (Bold Ruler) can't trot until he's warmed up. The doctor explained to me that the muscles in his back aren't attached in quite the usual way, but I don't

understand about that. He's a long striding runner and the most powerful striding horse I ever saw when he walks: Reaches out and plants his feet like this."

One can only sympathize with Smith that he did not even attempt to describe how an octogenarian with a bent spine might have tried to imitate a powerful racehorse.

Given such comment, it is no wonder that the legend of Bold Ruler has been handed down with an accompanying presumption that he was treated with Butazolidin.

Ogden Mills (Dinny) Phipps, a grandson of Mrs. Phipps who succeeded his father as chairman of The Jockey Club, said in 2005: "I've heard all my life that Bold Ruler ran on Butazolidin, but I can't tell you whether it is true or false."

Among veterinarians who were around the racetrack in Bold Ruler's day is Dr. Robert Copelan. He verified that it was widely spoken of that Bold Ruler received Bute but emphasized that he never had a direct connection to the colt.

Butazolidin is a subject that has generated opinion and emotion for a half-century or so. As Copelan — a founding member of the American Association of Equine Practitioners — recalled, Bute came into the realm of veterinary knowledge about 1955. It was produced by Geigy, a Swiss firm, and was developed for use on humans. He said the drug produced a rare idiosyncratic response called aplastic anemia in people and some years later was taken off the market for humans.

It was, however, helpful to horses.

"It is a non-steroidal anti-inflammatory, and to this day it is the monarch" of relief for soreness in horses, Copelan said in 2005.

Thinking back to the 1950s, Copelan realized that he and other veterinarians probably over-prescribed Bute while developing knowledge about the product but stressed that it was not illegal.

The stigma that later was applied to its use was seemingly non-existent in Bold Ruler's day.

John Jacobs, trainer of classic winners Personality and High Echelon, has specific memory of comments by his father, Hall of Fame trainer and champion Thoroughbred breeder Hirsch Jacobs, about Bold Ruler and Butazolidin, from as early as the Preakness.

"There are certain memories that just stick with

you," Jacobs said in 2005, thinking back to the Bold Ruler era. "Eddie Arcaro was very friendly with my father. He told my father that Bold Ruler was stiff as board when he ran in the Derby and that Mr. Fitz had told him 'you're going to see a different horse on Saturday (Preakness Day).' Arcaro said Mr. Fitz had given him (Bold Ruler) some medication.

"I did not hear that myself; I heard it from my father. But I was there in the paddock one day when my father said to Mr. Fitz that, 'I heard you gave Bold Ruler something.' Mr. Fitz said that was true, that 'it's something [with a name] like "beaut".' "

By 1960 the medication had become controversial, but even then, top-class stables and racetracks continued to hold the policy that its use was helpful and not improper. For example, *The Blood-Horse* of July 23, 1960, published a note, without comment, that Claiborne Farm's "Dunce, second in the Equipoise Mile, was on the Butazolidin list." Clearly, Bute was a medication that many felt was a good thing.

During that same year, however, controversy grew about Bute insofar as its being perceived as giving an unnatural edge to horses. The pendulum, and racing rules, swung against it, and Bute was a culprit in perhaps the most famous medication case in racing history. In 1968 Dancer's Image was disqualified from his victory in the Kentucky Derby because of a positive for Butazolidin, which by then had been banned in the state.

Over succeeding years, however, rules were altered specifically to allow use of a medication that Sunny Jim Fitzsimmons apparently had discerned as useful as early as the 1950s.

Fitzsimmons was not unfamiliar with practical day-to-day medications. He tinkered with an existing product known as Bigeloil — "90 percent alcohol" according to Jack Fitzsimmons — added some ingredients, and produced a commercial form that would keep a horse's legs tight but not cause blistering, even when bandages were applied and air kept out. Later, another similar but stronger formula was marketed under the name Fitzsimmons Leg Paint, which was intended to blister legs, a time-honored treatment for bucked shins. Fitzsimmons family descendants continued to own and operate the company producing these products until three or four years ago, Jack Fitzsimmons told us.

However, in August 1957, the reported problems from which Bold Ruler might have been suffering gave way to equally unspecific explanations of their having vanished. Charles Hatton, summarizing the year in the *American Racing Manual,* was content to bypass the subject as follows: "... every horseman who observed him (Bold Ruler) under saddle in the mornings was prepared to say that he was palpably sore. He looked and worked in a manner to refute this completely. And one could only concur in his handlers' explanation that the muscles over his croup were not attached in the normal way."

Even as ardent a Turf commentator as Joe Estes, then editor of *The Blood-Horse,* seemed so confounded by various reports that in *American Race Horses of 1957* he danced around several subjects in one paragraph and then let the matter drop: "For the next two months [after the Belmont Stakes], Bold Ruler needed nursing more than training. He got a severe reaction from encephalitis vaccine. He passed up the Arlington Classic because of being 'too tired too long' after a workout. He had a splint on his left foreleg, and as soon as that was corrected he began to show a mysterious sort of lameness which was traced to a 'nerve condition' in the right shoulder. The trouble eventually disappeared without ever having been diagnosed, and when Bold Ruler reappeared at Belmont Park after a rest at Saratoga he was loaded for bear."

Whatever Estes' account might have lacked in medical specifics, he surely had the last part dead on.

On September 9, nearly three months after the Belmont Stakes, Bold Ruler reappeared for the Times Square Handicap at Belmont Park. Despite its distinguished name, this was only a six-furlong overnight race, but Bold Ruler gave it glamour. Assigned 128 pounds, he dashed home by five and a half lengths over a high-class old rival in Greek Game (121) in 1:10 1/5. Cohoes was also in the beaten field.

The Times Square was run on Monday, and Bold Ruler's next race, the one-mile Jerome, was up on Saturday. Weights for the Jerome were not set until a few hours after the Times Square, which gave racing secretary Jimmy Kilroe a chance to react to Bold Ruler's dashing comeback. Kilroe gave him 130 — a traditional threshold for "weight-carriers" — and might have thought he was issuing a challenge.

Bold Ruler and Ogden Phipps' Bureaucracy formed a 1-5 entry for the Jerome. Bold Ruler proved amenable to being rated in third early as the handsomely named — but not equally endowed — Winged Mercury led Greek Game for a half-mile. Bold Ruler soon took over and drew off to win by six lengths as Bureaucracy moved up to finish second. The time for the historic mile race (dating from 1866) was in the range of brilliance that followers of Bold Ruler had come to expect — 1:35. The Belmont Park track record, only one-fifth of a second swifter, had been set by the sensational Count Fleet at two in 1942 and matched by the less renowned but speedy Blessbull in 1956.

This led to a meeting of giants, a theme visited upon Bold Ruler over and over. The Woodward Stakes was a weight-for-age event at one and a quarter miles that had been inaugurated in 1954, the year after its namesake, Mr. Fitz' old Belair Stud patron William Woodward Sr., had passed away.

In 1957 the Woodward brought championship contenders Bold Ruler, Gallant Man, and Dedicate into the same starting gate. The only other starter was an accomplished stakes winner named Reneged, like

Dedicate an older runner facing the two sprightly three-year-olds. The older pair carried 126 pounds each; the youngsters, 120.

Despite his strong feelings that fighting Bold Ruler had messed up his Kentucky Derby, Arcaro found himself slipping back into the mindset of trying to rate him when again faced with one and a quarter miles. Perhaps he was beguiled by Bold Ruler having rated kindly early in the Jerome.

In the Woodward, Arcaro tugged Bold Ruler back off the pace of Reneged, a 17-1 shot who led through fractions of :47 1/5 and 1:11. After six furlongs, Reneged still had a length lead, but in the next quarter-mile Bold Ruler took over and turned for home leading by two and a half lengths. The mile time of 1:36 was slightly slower than his standard fare, but he was not strong enough to forestall what would happen next. Bill Hartack had kept the five-year-old Dedicate along the rail, and he continued down there as he powered past Bold Ruler. Gallant Man also made his late run and relegated the Wheatley colt to third place but could only get to within a length and a half of the victorious Dedicate. The winner finished powerfully

enough to win in time of 2:01 for the ten furlongs.

Later, Arcaro conceded that "even in the Woodward I fought him a little too much." He was beaten three and a half lengths.

While Bold Ruler and Gallant Man were stars in the more glamorous three-year-old division, Dedicate was a highly accomplished older horse, and losing to him was no indication that the youngsters were of less quality than many had perceived them.

Fitzsimmons kept Bold Ruler active. Less than two weeks after the Woodward, he gave the natural flyer a chance to show his sheer speed, dropping him back to seven furlongs for the Vosburgh Handicap. Kilroe again assigned the colt 130 pounds, although he was facing older horses. Bold Ruler gave thirteen pounds of actual weight to the nice four-year-old Tick Tock, winner of the Sysonby and Sport Page handicaps that year amid a career of ten stakes victories.

Bold Ruler caught a sloppy track, a circumstance known to him only once before, when he lost his comeback race the previous fall. Nonetheless, he was sent off at 2-5. He was away with the pace, established a lead with a half-mile in :45, was in front by five after six furlongs in 1:08 4/5, and sailed on to win by nine in 1:21 2/5. In 1906, the second year of Belmont Park's existence, the powerhouse Roseben had set the track mark at 1:22, and it held up for more than fifty years until Bold Ruler took it down in the Vosburgh. (Bold Ruler's six-furlong fraction that day was a full second swifter than the official track record for that distance.)

Kilroe upped the weight to 133 pounds for the one and one-sixteenth-mile Queens County Handicap at Jamaica ten days later. Bold Ruler was 1-4. Arcaro let him roll and Bold Ruler quickly took a four-length lead. This grew to six lengths at the furlong pole, after which the jockey geared him down to win by two and a half lengths from the very good three-year-old Promised Land, to whom he was giving twenty-two pounds. The six-furlong clocking of 1:10 3/5 and final time of 1:42 4/5 might appear pedestrian, but at Jamaica, Blessbull's record for the one and one-sixteenth miles was only four-fifths faster. Hatton described Bold Ruler's Queens County performance as "breathtaking" and pointed out in his annual review that Promised Land went on to win four stakes on successive Saturdays that November, climaxed by a victo-

ry over Swoon's Son in the Pimlico Special.

John Jacobs, son of Promised Land's trainer and co-owner, Hirsch Jacobs, recalled the day of the Queens County: "I was driving my father to the racetrack, and he said, 'The gray horse (Promised Land) is really good right now. If Bold Ruler can beat him giving him all the weight, he would have to be a really good horse.'

"Well, Promised Land made a run at him, but Bold Ruler beat him easily. My father said, 'Geez, that is a hell of a great horse.' "

As for his own impression of Bold Ruler, John Jacobs thought back nearly fifty years and still concurred: "He was without doubt one of the best horses I ever saw. He was a super horse."

Next up was a trip to New Jersey's Garden State Park for the one and one-sixteenth-mile Benjamin Franklin Handicap on November 2. Ty Shea was the racing secretary at Garden State, and with Bold Ruler entered only against moderate three-year-olds, he burdened the colt with 136 pounds. The *Racing Form* summary said "breezing all the way" after Bold Ruler, again on a sloppy track, led by nine, eleven, and fourteen lengths at the points of call and glided home by twelve.

He gave twenty-seven pounds to runner-up Sarno. The time of 1:44 1/5 was more than two seconds over the track record.

The racing public clearly welcomed another meeting of the top three-year-olds Bold Ruler and Gallant Man, while Round Table had earned his way into that company as well. The Derby third-place finisher, Round Table had traipsed across the country on his eleven-race winning streak, switching without problem from dirt to turf and back, beating older horses along the way. His victory skein included the Hollywood Gold Cup, Westerner Stakes, United Nations Handicap, and Hawthorne Gold Cup.

The three sophomore colts had upheld very well the idea that the three-year-old crop was exceptional — even without the further help of Gen. Duke and in the face of Iron Liege's inability to build much upon his Kentucky Derby. If the three could be brought together for one meeting, the winner quite likely would be voted the three-year-old championship. If Dedicate were along for the ride, too, it would be even better.

Things came together quickly, and the Trenton Handicap at Garden State Park got its big three match-

up, but at the expense of another race. John D. Schapiro had invited Dedicate, Gallant Man, and Round Table to his Washington, D.C., International. However, Dedicate had been unplaced in the only two grass races of his career, and Gallant Man had never run on the turf. They declined, and so did Travis Kerr, whose Round Table was certainly not intimidated by the idea of running on Laurel's grass but who by running in that race would likely sacrifice his chance to move to the top of the Big Three. Dedicate's trainer, Carey Winfrey, decided his horse needed freshening and did not run him in either race.

In the meantime, Shea had issued weights for the Trenton Handicap, a $75,000 race of one and a quarter miles that somewhat magically was at the right place at the right time. He gave Dedicate 128, Gallant Man and Round Table 124 each, and Bold Ruler 122. Parsing this ranking, it placed Dedicate, Gallant Man, and Round Table above scale while placing Bold Ruler exactly at scale. The Jockey Club weight scale for one and a quarter miles in November called for 126 pounds on older horses, 122 on three-year-olds.

A crowd of 39,077 turned out for the three-horse

race. (Two other horses, King Ranch's Beam Rider [110] and Sam Tufano's Wise Margin [115], had been entered, but their owners recognized they might detract from the Big Three's showdown and announced the previous afternoon that their entries would not run.) Bettors collectively were at odds on their opinions, which reflected why the race was so fascinating. Even though only three horses were running, they were so evenly matched in public opinion that the track allowed place betting as well as win betting. Gallant Man wound up the slight choice at 1.40-1, Bold Ruler was 1.60-1, and Round Table 1.70-1.

Round Table's trainer, Willie Molter, like Fitzsimmons, came from a background and philosophy of busy campaigning, and he had given Round Table a prep over the track in an allowance race of one mile and seventy yards eight days earlier. Round Table won easily over a sloppy track that day, but for the Trenton the track was just wet enough to be labeled "good," which seemed to exploit the one weakness Round Table at times would exhibit. Gallant Man had run once since the Woodward, adding to his stature with a handy victory over the good older horse Third Brother in the two-mile Jockey Club Gold Cup.

Mrs. Phipps remained at her home in Palm Beach[1] and Mr. Fitz did not feel up to making the trip. Both had sons representing them: Ogden Phipps in the owner's camp, John Fitzsimmons for the trainer. Actually, the trainer's side had several compatriots. Bart Sweeney, one of Sunny Jim's assistants, saddled the colt, and son Jim Fitzsimmons was also there as well as John's daughter Kathleen.

Charles Hatton later recalled asking John Fitzsimmons if his father had left any special instructions to pass along to Arcaro. He was told that "No" had been the immediate answer, but the old man had quickly appended, "You might just remind him that it is a mile and a quarter."

To an outsider, that might have been the last thing you wanted to say to Arcaro, for it might play with his mind and have him falling back on the thought that somehow he had to conserve the big colt's speed.

Those on the inside probably knew of Arcaro's confidence, bordering on bravado. In the Trenton, the supposed strategy of the others would be to sit off Bold Ruler and be ready to take advantage of his anticipated weakening in the latter stages of a one and a quarter-mile race. Arcaro, however, told Whitney Tower, "I don't think this horse was ever as strong or as sound as he is right now. Furthermore, I know he can get the distance ... The answer to riding this dude is not to raise up and fight him in any way. Just drop your hands on him and he's going to lope along without any fight."

While Arcaro deservedly was renowned as "the Master," these comments rang similar to his observations prior to the Belmont.

Meanwhile, others saw the danger in letting Bold Ruler have his way. "If he ever gets five or six lengths in front, it'll all be over," said Gallant Man's trainer, John Nerud. Round Table's Molter agreed: "Once he gets in front by that far he just seems to float along and there's no catching him."

Arcaro knew the score: "The other boys won't let me wing off to any big lead — but if they do they'll sure be sorry."

The delicate strategy of Shoemaker on Gallant Man and Bill Harmatz on Round Table was to keep Bold Ruler under pressure but without using his own horse enough that the front two set it up for the third to come along and take all the marbles. As it turned out, Nerud's and Molter's nightmare scenario became an afternoon reality.

As he had been before the Preakness, Bold Ruler was warmed up before the race. The colt was jogged under tack from the barn to the paddock. At the start Bold Ruler rushed to the front. Although he was said in the charts to have a "snug hold," Arcaro was true to his word in terms of letting the colt have his way. The rider gave little hint of a "strategy," save for niggling the colt over to what he regarded as the best path in the footing. Bold Ruler raced a quarter-mile in :23 3/5, a half-mile in :47 1/5, and six furlongs in 1:11 1/5.

Quite probably, the key element in the race's failing to develop into a competition was Round Table's inability to handle the footing confidently. "This little horse just couldn't handle the going," Harmatz said. "He slipped and he slid. Every now and then he'd hit a dry spot and run a little. But when Bold Ruler started pulling out in the backstretch, I knew I was in trouble."

Excuses such as this are proffered in many circumstances and often arouse as much cynicism as sympathy. Round Table, however, was a great little horse, one that answered more questions about speed, class, courage, weight-carrying ability, and soundness than most other horses in history — read career record forty-three wins in sixty-six starts, record earnings of $1,749,869, victories under as much as 136 pounds, multiple championships, Horse of the Year status. If Harmatz said the colt could not get hold of the track, we are willing to accept this as told.

After six furlongs Round Table was second, but eight lengths behind Bold Ruler. With Round Table unable to act as a stalker, Shoemaker was left toothless aboard Gallant Man. Despite his early sprint victories, the colt had morphed into a runner whose main weapons were stamina and class, not early speed and class. Although he could tell that Round Table was unable to play the role of stalker, Shoemaker did not think Gallant Man was a horse he should hustle up to take on the role himself. As Arcaro had said, "the other boys" were very sorry but they had no cause to be remorseful. It was not, after all, by any blunder on their parts that they were quickly doomed to defeat.

Nevertheless, Gallant Man gave an impressive effort. From more than ten lengths off the pace after

six furlongs, he hurried along in the next quarter-mile to close to within three and a half lengths of the leader. Bold Ruler completed a mile in 1:36 4/5, and in his fourth attempt at one and a quarter miles or more, he for the first time had the situation under control.

Bold Ruler soared on alone and won by two and a quarter lengths. The nine-furlong clocking was 1:49 3/5 or two and one-fifth seconds slower than the track record for that distance. The final time for the one and a quarter miles was 2:01 3/5, only three-fifths of a second slower than Social Outcast's track record.

Asked to dissect the event, Arcaro chided the questioners happily: "You're making a big problem out of something that was awfully easy. I didn't think they could let me get so far in front. I thought they'd be on me from the half-mile pole on, but they weren't. I stayed out from the rail toward the middle of the racetrack because the going was better there."

On the other hand, he did make comments at odds with his confident pre-race comments: "The only doubt I had was about him going a mile and a quarter. We knew he could beat these horses as far as he could go."

After the race, the various relatives of owner and

trainer sought to make contact. In today's world, one can picture Ogden Phipps and John Fitzsimmons in the winner's circle, chins down, talking into cell phones. In 1957, however, telephones at the racetrack were a scarce commodity reflecting Wire Act fears of betting information flowing to the wrong parties.

Ogden Phipps presumably would have had access to call from track owner Gene Mori's office. "I'm going to get on the phone as soon as I can and call my mother," he said in the winner's circle. "The message will be, 'you won.' "

John Fitzsimmons' daughter Kathleen had the honors of calling Sunny Jim back on Long Island. The old fellow reacted to the news like a true horseman. As Red Smith quoted it, the sequence was this—

Excitable granddaughter: "Grandfather! He won!"

Very experienced old horseman: "How far?"

Excitable granddaughter: "I don't know. He won. Four lengths maybe."

Very experienced old horseman: "Did Eddie give him a breather on the turn, and then set him down?"

Granddaughter beginning to feel out of her depth: "I-I guess so. "

Very experienced old horseman: "Good. Those were his instructions."

The fractions would indicate that Eddie did as told: :23 3/5, :23 3/5, :24, :25 3/5, :24 4/5.

So, seemingly the trainer did have some specific orders for the jockey, despite what had been conveyed to the press.

Fitzsimmons did not automatically rule out Bold Ruler's racing again that year if a suitable meeting with Dedicate and Gallant Man developed. This did not happen.

In the meantime, racing secretary Kilroe helped Bold Ruler achieve a record without the colt's leaving his stall. He assigned Bold Ruler 139 pounds for each of two races. One, the Knickerbocker Handicap, came up the same day as the Trenton and so was obviously not in the cards. The second, the Roamer Handicap, came up the next week and received a "thanks, but no thanks." The 139-pound assignments were thought to be the highest ever assigned a three-year-old. The weight was one pound over the 138 that Man o' War carried in winning the Potomac Handicap at three in 1920.

For the second year in a row, voters in championship polls had to decide what to do with Bold Ruler. Despite having won, finally, at one and a quarter miles, he got his own way on that occasion, and it could still be reasonably conjectured that ten-furlong prowess was not one of his stronger weapons. One could cite Gallant Man for more positive stamina and Round Table for a longer winning streak. Still, it apparently was not particularly comfortable to vote for either of them coming off defeat in what was billed a year-end showdown. In the end, both of the major polls then extant, those conducted by *Daily Racing Form* and the Thoroughbred Racing Associations, designated Bold Ruler as the champion three-year-old. The highest honor, Horse of the Year, was divided. The *Form* poll voted Bold Ruler Horse of the Year, while the TRA elected Dedicate.

Gallant Man was shut out of a championship, while Round Table had grass to fall back on and was voted champion in that division for the first of three consecutive seasons.

Daily Racing Form and *Morning Telegraph* contracted with Garden State racing secretary Ty Shea to compile separate Free Handicaps for three-year-olds and for

older horses, in collaboration with the editors of the two trade dailies. The handicaps were based on a hypothetical race at one and one-eighth miles, to be run in December, and the judges were asked to look at overall 1957 performances without weighting late season races as more or less important than earlier ones.

Because the distance was nine furlongs, not ten, it must have been relatively easy to put Bold Ruler on top, at 130 pounds, which they did in the three-year-old male handicap. Gallant Man and Round Table each received 128; Gen. Duke, 127; and Iron Liege, 124.

Bold Ruler had won eleven of sixteen races; finished second twice, third twice, and fourth once; and earned $415,160.

Following the Trenton, Arcaro had issued as strong a benediction — albeit qualified — as Bold Ruler had ever received:

"For the things he can do, Bold Ruler is better than Nashua. This is a high-class horse. In fact, he's grade A."

As the Wheatley horses headed back to Florida, once again Sunny Jim and Gladys Phipps had a champion on their hands.

CHAPTER 9

A Campaign Delayed

From the time Bold Ruler got back to the races after his summer problems at three, everything had gone perfectly, aside from his defeat in the Woodward. At least, this is true insofar as the public record is concerned. Whatever soundness problems the stable had to combat, it seems unlikely that Fitzsimmons missed any targets he had eyed during that run of seven races in two months (September 9–November 9). One big traditional race he did miss was the Jockey Club Gold Cup, but given the dicey aspects of getting one and a quarter miles out of Bold Ruler, one can only conjecture that Mrs. Phipps and Mr. Fitz had no designs on a two-mile race.

Once the horse was back in Florida, the rosiness of the scenario quickly was replaced by more publicly announced problems.

The $100,000-added Widener Handicap was the centerpiece for the older male division at Hialeah, and several lesser handicaps laid out a path toward it. Mr. Fitz planned to run Bold Ruler in the seven-furlong Palm Beach Handicap and the one and one-eighth-mile McLennan Handicap in preparing for the one and a quarter-mile Widener.

On January 25, four days before the Palm Beach, the Wheatley camp announced in the jargon of the backstretch that Bold Ruler again had "popped a splint." The bony growth appeared in this case on the left hind leg. Fitzsimmons had to skip the Palm Beach and McLennan but was able to resume preparing the colt for the Widener. The wily trainer found himself in the same position as two years earlier when he had debuted Nashua in the Widener at four rather than following a prep.

Alas, only four days out, on February 18, Bold Ruler wrenched his left front ankle. The ankle filled, and Fitzsimmons had to announce his colt's withdrawal from the Widener. A month later, all was still not well. On March 21, Whitney Tower filed the following to the *Sports Illustrated* office:

"Sunny Jim Fitzsimmons is shipping Bold Ruler from Hialeah to New York's Belmont Park tomorrow, and there is, unfortunately, a distinct possibility that 1957's Horse of the Year may be finished for good. Fitz is unhappy about the colt's condition, which he describes as a sort of bursitis in the left foreleg. Bold Ruler has kept up in his training and when he finishes a work there is little or no swelling in the leg. However, after each night in his stall, his leg swells up a little and, despite X-ray therapy treatments, they don't seem to be able to keep the swelling down or make it disappear."

Furthermore, Mr. Fitz was quoted by Tower that, "When we get back to Belmont I'm going to put a real good work into this horse and see how he stands up to it. If he doesn't come out of it in good shape the only thing we can do is stop him. And I'm afraid that if we stop him it will be for a very long time. So long, in fact, that he probably wouldn't get back to the races this season — and next season I understand they want him to be retired to stud."

Such ominous interim announcements can be expected to lead to the news that the horse in ques-

tion has indeed been retired, and for the very good reason that his owners and trainers do not want to take chances with the animal's soundness. In Bold Ruler's case, this concern was certainly uppermost in the minds of Mrs. Phipps and Mr. Fitz, too, but again matters came right and Bold Ruler was sound and healthy enough to proceed on a similar run as the previous fall campaign — before anything went majorly wrong again.

Bold Ruler was judged able to make his first start as a four-year-old in mid-May. Fitzsimmons chose the six-furlong Toboggan Handicap on May 17, slightly more than six months since the colt had last competed.

Racing secretary Kilroe started Bold Ruler off with 133 pounds, which presaged some very burdensome weights in the bigger handicaps that lay ahead. Mrs. Phipps, regardless of her status as a Palm Beach resident, was really a New York owner when it came to the philosophies and traditions surrounding her stable. She had for years raced her horses in important New York handicaps, accepting weights that came her horses' way and probably admiring other owners' runners that she saw take up exceptional handicap assignments. Now, she had a horse worthy of such assignments, and she and Mr. Fitz took the tack that this was just part of campaigning a wonderful colt.

As a sign of the times, a Saturday crowd of 37,505 turned out to see Bold Ruler's comeback. The Toboggan was run down the old, diagonal Widener Chute that sliced across the Belmont Park infield. At the start Egotistical (113 pounds) might have figured a twenty-pound pull in weights was not sufficient advantage, for he swerved over, causing Arcaro to check Bold Ruler. Egotistical surged to the front, and Bold Ruler was still only third after a half-mile in :44 3/5. Egotistical fell back, but Clem came along strongly to take the lead from Tick Tock. They had daylight on Bold Ruler at the furlong pole, and the 2-5 favorite was under "strong handling," read the chart notes, in order to come along and beat Clem (117) by a half-length in 1:09. (It would seem a luxurious margin on a later day.) Tick Tock was third.

Mr. Fitz was venerated enough in racing, especially in New York, that he surely could have asked for special accommodations, for his severely bent posture

made it difficult for him to watch races. The *New York Times* report on the Toboggan by William Conklin would indicate that Fitzsimmons was loathe to ask for special treatment. The article also gives a fascinating insight into the old gentleman's day at the races, at least on that occasion:

"Mr. Fitz watched the race from a spot on the lawn between the clubhouse marquee and the trainers' stand. 'Can't see much of it from here,' he said, 'maybe the last quarter of a mile. I've got some glasses here — they help some but they're just a little better than nothing.'

" 'Going to make it to the winner's circle?' asked a well-wisher.

" 'Hope the horse does,' Sunny Jim replied. 'I know I'm not going to make it. I can't stand up around here as much as I used to.'

"While the field was going to the post, the dean of American trainers was concerned about his 2 1/2-year-old granddaughter, Dotty May, who had found something to cry about. He produced a few pennies to dry the tears, turned his head up the Widener stretch, and said: 'Well, I guess they're about ready to go.' "

At one point during the minute-plus that the race required, Fitzsimmons remarked: "He's running nice and clear. They can run at him, but I don't think they'll beat him. He's good right now and certainly ready to run his race."

A few moments later the trainer of the champion racehorse in America asked, "Did they put up the numbers? Somebody might have got to him just there at the end."

Informed that the numbers, and more importantly the right number, had been posted, Fitzsimmons gave little hint of celebration, more a sigh of relief.

"I'll be going along now," he said, "for I want to be back at the barn when he comes back. I want to see that he came out of it all right."

In twenty-first-century racing Mr. Fitz would presumably have watched the race in more comfortable circumstances, perhaps on a monitor in the Trustees' Room or in the executive offices, but he still would have hustled back to the barn to check on his horse.

Two weeks later, on Memorial Day weekend, the seven-furlong Carter Handicap was scheduled. The Carter presented the next step toward the assumed

path of top Eastern handicap horses of the era, i.e., the New York Handicap Triple Crown — the one-mile Metropolitan Handicap, one and a quarter-mile Suburban Handicap, and one and three-sixteenths-mile Brooklyn Handicap.

The Carter brought a meeting with Gallant Man, who also had had problems that cancelled his Florida winter appearances and who was making his comeback start at four. Figuring seven furlongs was more Bold Ruler's game than Gallant Man's, Kilroe put 135 pounds on the Wheatley colt, 128 on the other. Bold Ruler was 4-5; Gallant Man, 7-2. The Carter had been run first in 1895, and only Tom Fool had ever won it under as much as 135 pounds. Bold Ruler was equal to matching that distinction, but he did not do it with raw speed alone. In fact, after getting off in front, he allowed himself to be taken back to third behind Mr. Turf (111) and Admiral Vee (116) after a half-mile in :45 3/5. Turning for home, he had regained command, and he held sway through the stretch, being eased right at the last and defeating Tick Tock (113) by one and a half lengths. Gallant Man closed to nip Mr. Turf by a nose for third. The time was 1:22 3/5.

On June 14 the season reached a more serious phase. Kilroe assessed Gallant Man as more dangerous at the extra-furlong distance of the Met Mile and upped his weight to 130 off his promising debut, while leaving Bold Ruler at 135. The highest impost anyone had ever carried successfully in the Metropolitan Handicap (inaugurated in 1891) was the 134 carried by Devil Diver (1944) in the second of his three consecutive Met Mile victories.

A one-mile race often elicits sprinters' speed but then requires a good bottom of stamina for the final wrenching furlong. Assessing the situation, bettors, while impressed by the champion, were wisely wary. Bold Ruler just barely was made odds-on, at 19-20 (his longest price of the year), and Gallant Man was sent off at about 3-1.

Bold Ruler found himself in front and was running into a headwind of twenty-five miles per hour down the backstretch. Shoemaker restrained Gallant Man some nine lengths off the pace with only one horse behind him, availing himself of the field as a windbreak. After a half-mile in :46 1/5, Bold Ruler had a one-length lead, and this had increased slightly to one

and a half lengths after six furlongs in 1:10 3/5. Although in the stretch he was racing with the wind as his ally, the same was true for the others. Gallant Man was still about seven lengths back but then swung off the rail and began closing rapidly. The previous year a pacemaker and twelve furlongs had appeared to cant matters in Gallant Man's favor. Now it was weight and wind that were against Bold Ruler, and, again, Gallant Man stormed right past him, drawing out to win by two lengths. Ultimately, of course, the real foe of Bold Ruler was the extreme quality of one Gallant Man.

Bold Ruler finished second by one and a half lengths over Clem (114), and Promised Land (118) was fourth. The time of 1:35 3/5 missed the Belmont Park record by four-fifths of a second.

Bold Ruler and Gallant Man thus had met eight times and each had finished ahead of the other four times. In outright victories when racing against each other, Bold Ruler owned four and Gallant Man two. They never met again. Bold Ruler continued on the path of the East's grinding handicap circuit, while Gallant Man ventured West for a stair-step of tests, the

Hollywood Gold Cup at one and a quarter miles and then the Sunset Handicap at one and five-eighths miles. Theoretically, California was Round Table territory, but by then Round Table had launched the Midwestern phase of his campaign. By the time Gallant Man and Round Table were back east, Bold Ruler had been retired by injury. Gallant Man's career came to a similar conclusion a month and a half later, and he and Round Table never met at four, either.

Fitzsimmons wanted a race for Bold Ruler during the three weeks between the Met Mile and the Suburban. He eyed two choices: the one and one-eighth-mile Stymie Handicap on June 25 and the seven-furlong Roseben Handicap on June 28. He was leaning toward the shorter race, perhaps because of its speed-sharpening potential, but the weights for the Roseben came out three days before the Stymie, and Bold Ruler got 138. The weight was 133 for the longer race, and Fitzsimmons took that choice. He and Mrs. Phipps were sporting, but they weren't foolhardy!

Bold Ruler led throughout the Stymie and rated along comfortably at Arcaro's gentle restraining. They rambled through six furlongs in 1:11 1/5, then kicked

in a nice quarter-mile in :24 1/5, for a mile in 1:35 2/5. This provided a six-length lead, and Bold Ruler finished five in front of Admiral Vee (112), with Pop Corn (108) third. Inside Tract (112) was among the others. The time of 1:48 2/5 reflected the goal of getting the race completed and won, without histrionics, but even so was only one and one-fifth seconds away from Gallant Man's track record.

CHAPTER 10

"Courage was mine"

—Wilfred Owen

In later years, as a televised racing commentator — highly knowledgeable but never experienced enough to seem truly comfortable on camera, Eddie Arcaro allowed the Kentucky Derby to dominate in his memory. He would say that Bold Ruler never got one and a quarter miles, although he in fact rode the horse to three major victories at the distance!

In some ways the most dramatic of those was next on the horizon. The Suburban Handicap came up about a week and a half after the Stymie, on the Fourth of July. Bold Ruler had done nothing to induce Kilroe to back off, and he was assigned 134 pounds going a distance that clearly was a challenge to him. Again, this feat called for historical context. In a race dating from 1884, Whisk Broom II had won the Suburban under

139 pounds in 1913, and the only other horse to carry more than 132 and win the race had been Grey Lag (135) in 1923.

As is always the case in such matters, the package of the top-weight is one measure, and the poundage being given away is another. In the 1958 Suburban Handicap, the differentials included concession of eighteen to Promised Land, twenty to Sharpsburg, twenty-four to Third Brother, twenty-five pounds to Clem, and twenty-nine to Beau Diable.

For the three years that Bold Ruler had been performing at the highest levels, Mrs. Adele Rand's Clem had been toiling against the top milieu without actually joining it. That was about to change. Winner of the Arlington Classic, Withers, and Shevlin at three, Clem clearly was developing toward his peak powers.

Despite the arduous assignment and his defeat in the Met Mile, Bold Ruler was 1-2. (At that time, one and a quarter-mile races at Belmont started from a chute that was an extension of the backstretch into the infield of the training track, which is set almost perpendicular to the clubhouse turn of the main track. After the break, the field made a gentle dogleg onto the backstretch proper, so ten furlongs was a one-turn affair. Today, as Breeders' Cup fans well know, the chute does not extend that far anymore, so a one and a quarter-mile race at Belmont starts via an angular placement of the gate halfway into the first turn.)

By the time of the Suburban, Arcaro could rate Bold Ruler to the degree that had caused man and horse some friction the previous year. Mindful of the weight, the great jockey took a long hold and had his star a length off the pace as they raced up the long backstretch. As they went into the turn, Arcaro sat down to riding, and his big fellow leapt out to a two-length lead. The fractions seem controlled but could be assessed as withering, when one considers the weight Bold Ruler was carrying — 1:10 3/5 for six furlongs and the ubiquitous "35" range for a mile, 1:35 1/5. That delivered Bold Ruler to the quarter-pole in front by two lengths, but this was Clem's spiritual proving ground, and he was about to exhibit a degree of manhood not necessarily expected of him.

For further explanation we happily yield to the emotive prose of Charlie Hatton, as preserved in the *American Racing Manual* of 1959:

"Clem was made of stern stuff. He came up fighting again in the stretch and thrust his head in front. Arcaro said later that he let his mount 'see Clem,' a daring and confident maneuver near the end of so important a race, 'and that made Bold Ruler mad.' ...

"The embattled Bold Ruler and Clem made a thrilling sight. The vast crowd present will cherish the picture they made as they fought it out, bobbing side by side in unison in that desperate struggle as one of the most gripping and dramatic reminiscences of their entire sporting repertory. Future posters should picture their forward-flung, lean heads, the flashing eyes and quivering nostrils."

Hatton continued: "With the finish 100 yards away, the choral roll of their flying hoofs, the slapping whips against the roar high in the stands, was like a song. It was now a question of sheer bulldog tenacity. The last desperate shred of their strength was expended in each headlong, straining bound. Their heads and tails were level with their backs. Aroused by the arrogance of the challenging Clem, Bold Ruler's whole being seemed to say, 'Back! Back! I am your master. I will race you to the death.'

"As the finish raced up, it was Bold Ruler's crimson nostrils that showed in front ... You can imagine the spontaneous cheering of those who had made him 1-2 in the Tote and who love a true Thoroughbred, one who had displayed such valor under fire. The time was 2:01, and times are believable at Belmont.[1] There have been slightly faster Suburbans, but none more soul-satisfying and epic as a dramatization of the Thoroughbred virtues.

"That day, surely, Bold Ruler was a great horse."

Tom Fool, Helioscope, and Nashua had won their Suburbans that decade in slightly faster times than Bold Ruler, but those horses had carried 128 pounds, not 134.

While this was an enormously important and impressive moment for Bold Ruler, it would take on added patina when Clem proceeded to underline his arrival as a major player by defeating Round Table in three consecutive meetings, climaxed by the Woodward at level weights.

While Hatton was up to describing the glory of the Suburban, he did not ignore the realities of life. A few paragraphs later, he recalled that Arcaro told Mr. Fitz

that the colt — in Hatton's words not Arcaro's — "put in some shockingly lame steps upon pulling up."

Nevertheless, the horse came out of the race in sufficiently good condition that, with Bigeloil, Bute, X-ray therapy — whatever — or just plain physical capacity, he was ready two weeks later for another go at one and a quarter miles, and again under 134 pounds. The challenge on July 19 was the Monmouth Park Handicap at Monmouth Park, a stylish New Jersey ocean-resort track where he had never raced before. While the Monmouth had a truncated history in comparison with the Suburban, it carried a significantly larger purse to the winner, $70,772 compared to $53,360. (The colt's only larger purses won in his career were $94,200 for his Flamingo Stakes at three and $91,145 for his Futurity at two.)

Once again, as an aid to working out any stiffness, Bold Ruler was ponied to the paddock under tack and rider.

The Monmouth Park Handicap originated in 1884 at the original Monmouth Park. It had ten runnings and then was resumed a half-century or so later, in 1946, when major racing returned to New Jersey. Helioscope had won under 131 pounds and Nashua under 129, so Bold Ruler was charting new waters with his 134.

If racing fans were prone to quibble about what Bold Ruler had proven in the Suburban, they might have leapt upon the fact that at Belmont Park one and a quarter miles was run around "one turn" and thus might be interpreted as less of a test than the same distance around "two turns." Monmouth, as a one-mile track, presented this distance in the two-turn scenario.

As is true of most mile tracks, a one and a quarter-mile race starts on a short chute that joins the homestretch. With an animal that can see pretty much all around him, as a horse can, it is not infrequent that the wide, sweeping turn for home that cuts into his vision to the left soon after the start beguiles the horse into thinking he/she is supposed to turn that way at that point. This happened briefly in Bold Ruler's Monmouth Park Handicap, for he broke quickly from the inside post position and so had no horse to his left in the early strides of the race.

Arcaro straightened him quickly, and Sharpsburg (113) moved up to track him in second. Bold Ruler had a one and a half-length lead after a half-mile in :48 and a length lead after six furlongs in 1:12. At that point Nick Shuk urged the 8-1 Sharpsburg up to attempt a challenge, and indeed he got to Bold Ruler's head after a mile in 1:36 2/5. Thereafter, as described in unusually descriptive chart notes, "Arcaro flicked him (Bold Ruler) once on the shoulder with the whip and scrubbed lightly through the final sixteenth, but Bold Ruler was in complete authority at all times and appeared to have something in reserve."

Sharpsburg finished second, beaten by three-quarters of a length while six lengths in front of third-placed Bill's Sky Boy, who got twenty-nine pounds from the winner. The persistent Third Brother (110) was fourth, followed by the accomplished King Ranch mare Dotted Line (102) and then Beam Rider (108).

The final time of 2:01 3/5 was two-fifths of a second slower than the track record, which Round View had held since 1947.

After Bold Ruler's three major weight-carrying feats, and victories, within about three weeks, Fitzsimmons immediately spoke in terms of skipping the following Saturday's Brooklyn Handicap to await the Whitney at Saratoga, where Bold Ruler had never gotten to race. He had hardly completed that comment before he quickly appended, "but don't count me out of the Brooklyn yet."

Fitzsimmons also said that the Monmouth Park Handicap "was a real hard race," somewhat contravening the chart-caller's interpretation. "If it wasn't for the weights there would have been no race. These handicaps are all tough."

Sharpsburg, who had been bred by Calumet Farm but was then owned by R.E. Faircloth's Fairlawn Farm, had developed into a nice sort at five that year, winning the Narragansett Special and three other stakes.

Arcaro said admiringly after the Monmouth Park Handicap that Bold Ruler "knows what to do and he seems to do it almost all the time. He tried to duck leaving the gate ... but once I straightened him out he knew where he was supposed to go."

Bold Ruler recovered from the Monmouth Park Handicap quickly and was sound enough that Fitzsimmons, in fact, did decide to run him back in the Brooklyn. If the trainer's comments about the severity of the Monmouth race, and of handicaps in general, had in anyway been directed toward the kind heart of

Jimmy Kilroe, they did not seem to hit their mark. Kilroe's compliment was 136 pounds for the Brooklyn Handicap. This resumed the same old theme of seeking context with historic achievements: The Brooklyn dated from 1887, and only Bold Ruler's grandsire Discovery in 1936 and New York Handicap Triple Crown winner Tom Fool in 1953 had ever won it under as much as 136 pounds.

The Brooklyn took Bold Ruler back to Jamaica, where his racing career had begun. There, too, it would end.

The crowd trusted Bold Ruler and made him 2-5, but he failed to make the lead and was some seven lengths back early. He manfully worked up to within one and a half lengths of the lead, but he was fouled by Sharpsburg, and then he failed to menace, finishing seventh in an eight-horse field, beaten fifteen lengths.

"He couldn't turn it on at any time in the race," Arcaro said. The winner, Greentree Stable's Cohoes (110), was another who had battled with the best without actually joining them. The Brooklyn, won in 1:55 3/5 (only two-fifths of a second off Lucky Draw's track record), launched him on a streak of four wins in five starts, including the Whitney and the Sysonby. Sharpsburg was disqualified from second for fouling Bold Ruler. All that, however, was beside the point.

The painful bursitis had turned up again in Bold Ruler's left front ankle. On August 4 came the announcement that he was being retired to stud.

"I could probably get him back to the races in the fall," Mr. Fitzsimmons said at the time, "but he's too valuable to take chances with, so we'll stop on him for good right now.

"He may have aggravated the ankle in the Brooklyn, or in training. I know that something happened to him, but I don't know when it happened or exactly what he's got."

Mrs. Phipps was in Europe at the time, so Fitzsimmons' direct discussions had been with her son, Ogden, who presumably was in contact with his mother.

Bold Ruler thus had won five of his seven races as a sterling handicapper and earned $209,994 that year. His overall record was twenty-three wins in thirty-three starts and earnings of $764,204, well under Nashua's millionaire status.

Bold Ruler had first been assigned that threshold of weight carriers, 130 pounds, with thirteen more races left in his career. In those thirteen starts he carried 130 or more in eleven races, winning all but two.

By year's end in 1958, Round Table had supplanted Nashua as the all-time leading money earner, and with another exemplary cross-country campaign, fourteen wins in twenty starts, he prevailed on both polls as champion older male and Horse of the Year. Round Table carried on at five to be co-champion handicap horse as well as champion turf horse for the third straight year.

Gallant Man, in his last year of racing, 1958, again was left out in the championship voting, despite his own weight-carrying and staying exhibitions. Bold Ruler got a consolation prize in voting at four, being named champion sprinter.

Oddly, it was easy to make a case that Bold Ruler was more distinguished in the year he did not win a share of the Horse of the Year championship than the previous year when he did, but there was no gainsaying that Round Table was a remarkable candidate as well.

The committee compiling the Free Handicap for the division countered with Bold Ruler and Gallant Man as equal top-weights at 132, Round Table at 131. Emphasizing the exalted sense surrounding those three, even as stellar a campaigner as Swoon's Son was ranked nine pounds lower, in fourth, with Clem at 122.

At the end of the twentieth century, *The Blood-Horse* convened a panel to assess the best horses of the hundred years just passed. Round Table was the most highly rated from the wonderful group of horses that ran in 1956–58 (himself, Bold Ruler, Gallant Man, and Gen. Duke). Round Table was placed seventeenth, Bold Ruler nineteenth, and Gallant Man again slipping down, to thirty-sixth. The brevity of Gen. Duke's career left him off the list, although the lingering memory of his Florida Derby certainly encouraged late evening "what-if?" discussions.

Writing in *American Race Horses of 1958,* Joe Estes, longtime editor of *The Blood-Horse,* wrote glowingly of the Wheatley champion:

"Bold Ruler was assured of a very high place among the best horses of the time. Not since the days of his maternal grandsire, Discovery, had an American horse

carried such high weights ... (Weight, of course, reflects on not only the class of the horse, but the class of the owner.) Bold Ruler's long series of mishaps and his unsoundness were in marked contrast to the amazing durability of Round Table, and the Wheatley star got only an even break in his eight contests with Gallant Man.

"But neither these nor any others of their age outshone him in the composite of virtues that make a race horse — speed, weight-carrying ability, courage under pressure, and versatility in adapting to varied track conditions."

The author has frequently counseled with himself — admittedly not the most productive of mental exertions — on the horses under question. We generally come to the conclusion that Bold Ruler was the most brilliant, Round Table the soundest and most durable, while Gallant Man was one running s.o.b. with exceptionally bad timing as to birth year.

Put them in a race of imagination — even weights, dry track, one and a quarter miles — and even Charlie Hatton would lack the words to describe it.

CHAPTER 11

"...a father unto many sons"

—Shakespeare

In the spring of 1959, Bold Ruler entered stud at his birthplace, Claiborne Farm. He clearly was a stallion prospect of impressive potential, son of a great sire and possessed of high speed, early maturity, and sufficient stamina for most of America's best races. His bottom line was not replete with the sorts of individuals that could cause it to be described as a "sire family," but only the fussiest pedigree elitist could readily pick apart Bold Ruler's credentials.

As soon as the first Bold Rulers hit the racetrack, his sire potential received an enhanced sense of verification. His first crop included seventeen foals, of which fifteen got to the races, fourteen won, and eight won stakes. That group included not only some late-developing types but also some that came running in a hurry. Among the first crop (two-year-olds of 1962), Speedwell (from the blue hen mare Imperatrice) won the Debutante at Churchill Downs in the spring for Chris Chenery's Meadow Stable; Wheatley's Bold Princess (from the blue hen mare Grey Flight) won the Schuylerville Stakes at Saratoga; and Ornamento won the Breeders' Futurity for John W. Galbreath's Darby Dan Farm.

Nevertheless, in his first "start" as a competitor on sire lists, Bold Ruler as a sire of juveniles in 1962 finished seventh. His own sire, Nasrullah, was first, represented by champion Never Bend. If one could ascribe human egos to such a situation, it is likely that Bold Ruler would have been most chaffed by knowing that Dedicate ranked just ahead of him.

The young Claiborne stallion would not be outpaced in sire statistics very often thereafter.

In 1963, with only two-year-olds and three-year-olds, Bold Ruler led the general sire list for the first time. Leadership among all sires was an aerie he would find so comfortable as to occupy it six more seasons in succession.

From his first crop, lovely Lamb Chop earned Bold

Ruler his first status as the sire of a champion, reigning in the three-year-old filly division in 1963 after victories in the Coaching Club American Oaks, Spinster Stakes, and seven other stakes. She raced in the colors of William Haggin Perry as part of his partnership with Claiborne Farm. Bold Ruler also led the list of sires of two-year-olds in 1963, for the first of six times.

Sunny Jim Fitzsimmons retired on June 23, 1963, so his seventy-eight years working around the races took him into the early days of the Bold Ruler era as a sire. (In 1887, as a teenager having battled a bout of malaria, Fitzsimmons was advised by a doctor in Long Branch, New Jersey, that a recent episode of heart palpitations indicated he should "give up racing. Stay away from that excitement or you won't last long with that heart." Fitzsimmons was more than seventy years in complying.) On June 15 of that year, King's Story (Bold Ruler—Narrative) won the Miss Woodford at Monmouth Park. Ah, Miss Woodford. For Sunny Jim, the name harked back to the mists of teenage struggle and wonder, a championship imprint when life was all about absorbing the imprint of dreams and fears and practicality.

Two days later Wheatley's Beautiful Day (Bold Ruler—Misty Morn) won the filly division of the National Stallion Stakes as Mr. Fitz's final stakes winner.

That spring Mr. Fitz had forewarned Ogden Phipps that it was too difficult to continue his daily routine. "This was a great blow to my mother and myself, who have had such a wonderful association with Mr. Fitz for 38 years," Phipps said at the time. "The record speaks for his skill as a trainer, but what has been more important for us has been Mr. Fitz the man, a man of great character whose outlook on life and concern for his fellow man endeared him to all fortunate enough to know him. He plans to be at our stable, often, and we certainly hope so."

Jack Fitzsimmons, a grandson, said he never was annoyed by the cartoon name of "Sunny Jim" for his grandfather. It seemed to fit his own image and memory of a singular figure: "I never saw him upset with anybody — unless they had put a bandage on incorrectly."

Whatever the job, a true pro is a true pro.

Mr. Fitz was succeeded by Bill Winfrey. Thus, the man who had trained Native Dancer, Next Move, Bed o' Roses, Social Outcast, Find, and other major horses for Alfred Vanderbilt, would be in on much of the early success of the young Bold Rulers.

The next year the Bold Ruler brigade picked up steam. From the first crop, the late-developing distaffer Batteur won a division of the Santa Margarita en route to a career of a half-dozen stakes wins in the Perry stable (trained by Jim Maloney). Farm records indicate that her dam, the Claiborne homebred champion Bayou, was the first mare covered by Bold Ruler, in 1959, and the last, in 1971.

Stunningly, Bold Ruler's two-year-old crop of 1964 included both the two-year-old colt champion, Bold Lad, and the two-year-old filly champion, Queen Empress. Both were bred and raced by Wheatley Stable and thus trained by Winfrey. As Mrs. Phipps' granddaughter Cynthia put it, the grande dame of the Turf might have projected a sense of reserve, but what fun it must have been to campaign those two.

In addition to four hard-fought stakes wins, Bold Lad (a son of champion Misty Morn) took the Hopeful Stakes and Champagne Stakes by seven lengths each, and he was ranked at 130 pounds on the Experimental Free Handicap. The rating matched those of Native

Dancer, Bimelech, and Alsab, and to this day has only been exceeded by Count Fleet's 132.

At three Bold Lad prompted a return to the Kentucky Derby. Cynthia Phipps recalls taking a train to Louisville with her grandmother but is not sure it was the last time Mrs. Phipps visited Kentucky. What is tough to forget, of course, is that a part of the stands burst into flames that day. It is perhaps too pat to say that Wheatley's hopes "went up in flames," too, but that is pretty much what happened. Bold Lad was injured during the running and struggled home tenth of eleven. He was away from the races for a year, but, despite the injury, his failure in the Derby was among the mental chips stacked up by observers to justify the growing prejudice that the Bold Rulers were ill-suited for one and a quarter miles, especially on the first Saturday in May of their three-year-old season.

Two years after Bold Lad, his full brother, Successor, matched his status as champion two-year-old. (That same year, Gladys Phipps' twin sister, Beatrice Lady Granard, had the champion two-year-old in England in the form of an Irish-bred Bold Ruler colt. She had named him "Bold Lad" in honor of Mrs. Phipps' earlier champion of the same name. Both Dinny Phipps and Cynthia Phipps recall that their grandmother was not at all pleased by this nominally confusing honor and made her sister aware of her feelings. Still "they were great friends, and Lady Granard used to come to stay with my grandmother for a month in Palm Beach each year," recalled Dinny. "They were opposites. My grandmother was an introvert, and her sister was an extrovert.")

In 1967, the year after Successor, Ogden Phipps — not for the first time — equaled his mother in a specific racing achievement when his Vitriolic was named champion two-year-old colt and his Queen of the Stage was named champion two-year-old filly. Both were by Bold Ruler.

Thus, the nationally reigning stallion had left a record for his family home team of five of the last eight champions in the juvenile ranks.

Many are the ways to illustrate the exceptional prowess of Bold Ruler as a stallion.

In terms of pure statistics, of course, he was the leading sire of earners in North America for seven years in succession (1963–69). This surpassed the records of his own sire, Nasrullah, and Bull Lea and

Star Shoot (five leaderships each), among North American stallions of the twentieth century. After his barn-mate Round Table[1] and a couple of others led the lists, Bold Ruler returned for another statistical leadership, in 1973, when his son Secretariat won the Triple Crown. He thus led the general sire list eight times — a modern record.

Bold Ruler came close to leading in nine seasons. In 1970 Hail to Reason led with $1,400,839 and Bold Ruler was second with $1,123,051.

Bold Ruler also continued to star as a sire of juveniles, leading that list in earnings six times between 1963 and 1972.

As the 1960s rushed by, it became a presumption that each new crop would bring one — or perhaps several — dazzling Bold Rulers out for racing glory, and for the best and most traditional stables.

In 1964 when the Bold Ruler juveniles Bold Lad and Queen Empress were their genders' champions, Bold Ruler also had the Sorority winner in Meadow Stable's Bold Experience and the Sanford winner in George D. Widener's Cornish Prince. In 1966, when victories in the Garden State and Champagne stakes solidified Successor's championship season, Widener's Bold Ruler colt Bold Hour won the Futurity and Hopeful, while the Phipps family's Bold Ruler colt Great Power won the Sapling and National Stallion stakes. In 1967, when Ogden Phipps' Bold Ruler pair of Vitriolic and Queen of the Stage were the two-year-old champions, their supporting group included Wheatley's Bold Ruler colt What a Pleasure, winner of the Hopeful, etc., and Meadow Stable's Syrian Sea, winner of the Selima, etc.

Even in years when some other sire slipped in a champion, Bold Ruler might still be a presence. For example, in 1968, Top Knight, by Vertex, was the top two-year-old, but the Bold Ruler ranks included Wheatley Stable's King Emperor (Laurel Futurity, Cowdin, and Sanford) and Ogden Phipps' Reviewer (Sapling and Saratoga Special).

Among other measures of Bold Ruler's status during the years his offspring were running was the Experimental Free Handicap. He was represented by two-year-olds for thirteen seasons, and he had one or more juveniles ranked in the top ten of their gender in ten seasons. On all but two of those handicaps, he had

more than one in the top ten.

Bold Ruler's half-dozen juvenile champions — Bold Lad, Queen Empress, Successor, Vitriolic, Queen of the Stable, and Secretariat — were top weights on the experimental handicaps. Insofar as volume is concerned, Bold Ruler's best statistics came in 1964, 1966, and 1967: In each of those years, a total four of the top ten on the experimental handicap (counting male and female top tens separately) were sired by the Wheatley phenomenon.

In the face of such dominance, it might seem bewildering that there was also a negative tide to Bold Ruler's march of dominance. As the recitation of Bold Ruler's racing career points out, doubts always lingered as to his ability to get one and a quarter miles, which is still the bespoken goal of American breeders and owners — however illogically they may act in seeking it.

Following the 1957 Kentucky Derby defeat of Bold Ruler himself, a sequence of Bold Ruler colts also failed in the Churchill classic. Well, it is deceptive to say "sequence," as if there were a sameness of qualifications and conditions.

As mentioned earlier, Bold Lad was injured in his

Derby but would likely have failed even if the race had been significantly shorter. In 1966 Wheatley Stable's Stupendous finished fourth in the Derby. Then came Successor, a disappointment at three, but one that did add a victory at one and five-eighths miles in the Lawrence Realization.

In short, the Kentucky Derby image of Bold Ruler was colored by relatively little evidence. Yet, we have to concede that his shortcomings were so commonly perceived that even his own stable encouraged skepticism.

In our interview with Ogden Phipps in 1989, that esteemed gentleman declined the opportunity to be an apologist for Bold Ruler. "Fitzsimmons said Bold Ruler was a faster horse and Nashua a better stayer," Phipps recalled. "A mile was Bold Ruler's distance. Arcaro said he'd never been on a horse that broke faster ... Like all good milers, if the race set up right, Bold Ruler could win at one and a quarter miles in good company." If that cool judgment survived three decades of memory after Bold Ruler's Suburban, we concluded it would be ungentlemanly to challenge it. After all, this was a grand old sportsman who had the capacity to revere other owners' horses as coolly as

his own. A few minutes later we heard this breeder and owner of Buckpasser and Easy Goer give some other stable's horse — Count Fleet — pride of place among his personal best champions of memory! Now, that's a sportsman.

Sunny Jim Fitzsimmons' attorney grandson Jack used a targeted phrase to underscore the generalizations: Mr. Fitz, he recalled, felt that "after a mile, Bold Ruler lost his 'acuteness.' " Now, that's a lawyer.

By the time Bold Ruler actually had a Derby winner, the sire was deceased. Furthermore, that son, Secretariat, was transcendent, so great and singular that it was hard to give credit to a sire in the thought that he "got horses like Secretariat ..." Similarly, one doubts that proponents of Fair Play in an earlier day would have referred to his offspring as "Man o' War, and horses like that."

The change of direction in the history of Bold Ruler and the Kentucky Derby — as the bellwether one and a quarter-mile race in America — began in 1970. That year, the Kentucky Derby winner was Dust Commander, whose sire, Bold Commander, was a nice sort of Wheatley Stable colt, but not one that Mrs.

Phipps would have pushed on Claiborne Farm to stand.

Bold Ruler's great son Secretariat followed in 1973, with his Derby record 1:59 2/5 en route to the first Triple Crown in twenty-five years. The very next year, the Derby's exalted one-hundredth running was won by Cannonade, whose sire, Bold Bidder[2], had been in the Wheatley Stable the year before Fitzsimmons retired and had become one of the oldster's personal favorites for later potential. The year 1975 found What a Pleasure, Wheatley Stable's 1967 Hopeful Stakes winner by Bold Ruler—Grey Flight, represented as the sire of the Derby winner in defending juvenile champion Foolish Pleasure.

In 1976 What a Pleasure had the strong Derby favorite in another defending juvenile champion, Honest Pleasure, but Honest Pleasure was upset in the Derby by Bold Forbes — son of the Wheatley-bred Bold Ruler stallion Irish Castle (another Hopeful winner)!

Three years later the great, four-time champion Spectacular Bid became the second Kentucky Derby winner for the stallion Bold Bidder. In the meantime, the Bold Ruler link had come through from greater distance when another four-time champion, Seattle Slew

— by Bold Reasoning, by Boldnesian, by Bold Ruler — had won the 1977 Derby en route to winning the Triple Crown while undefeated. In 1984 Claiborne Farm's homebred Swale, son of Seattle Slew, added one more sweet chapter to this irony in winning his own Derby and Belmont.

Bold Ruler, who failed to win the Derby in 1957, had surely established his ghost in the spiritual bell tower of the Twin Spires.

At the end of the twentieth century, *The Blood-Horse* poll, which ranked Bold Ruler nineteenth, placed two of his male-line descendants well above him, with Seattle Slew ninth and Spectacular Bid tenth.

Overall, Bold Ruler sired eighty-two stakes winners, for a superb 22 percent from foals. His daughters produced 119 stakes winners.

Bold Ruler sired ten North American champions: Lamb Chop, Bold Lad, Queen Empress, Gamely, Successor, Vitriolic, Queen of the Stage, Bold Bidder, Secretariat, and Wajima. The Irish Bold Lad qualified as an eleventh champion.

The logistics surrounding a great stallion were far different in Bold Ruler's time from those that prevail today. Depending on management's philosophy, a horse with the record and sizzle of a Bold Ruler might cover more than two hundred mares a year in two hemispheres in 2005. In Bold Ruler's day, custom and a lesser-developed ability to discern optimal stages for a mare to be covered, created a concept of proper husbandry that meant the eight-time leading sire never was represented by more than thirty-five foals in any crop.

Moreover, the commercial scene did not guarantee that the most fashionable stallion would see sons and daughters lining up at Keeneland, or Fasig-Tipton, or Newmarket. Bold Ruler's first foals were yearlings in 1961 and his last foals were yearlings in 1973. Yet, only twenty-five Bold Ruler yearlings were sold at auction. They averaged a handsome figure for the era, $119,164, and two of them brought all-time records — One Bold Bid for $170,000 at the 1964 Keeneland July sale and 1975 sophomore champion-to-be Wajima for $600,000 at the 1973 Keeneland July sale.

By 1968 Bold Ruler had such status that the Phippses asked Bull Hancock to put into place an arrangement whereby they could plug in to other breeders' distinguished broodmare bands, which

would not be available to them otherwise. The plan was to invite owners of great mares and potentially great mares to breed to Bold Ruler for two years (or until the arrangement produced two foals), without any fee being paid. "Our deal with most people," Ogden Phipps recalled years later, "was that, 'if the first foal is a colt you get it, and if it's a filly we get it.' "

The most famous outcome of these assignations was, of course, connected to the Chenery mare Somethingroyal, who had already foaled a classy Bold Ruler filly in Syrian Sea. Dinny Phipps bought a season from his grandmother to allocate to Somethingroyal, who was also the dam of Sir Gaylord. When returned to Bold Ruler under the dual-season scheme, Somethingroyal foaled a filly first and a colt second. The colt was Triple Crown winner Secretariat and went to the Chenerys; the filly was The Bride, who was later a stakes producer for Dinny Phipps. Although, as Ogden Phipps had explained, for the most part the deal was that the Phippses got the first foal from the two-year deal if it were a filly, the specifics of the Bold Ruler—Somethingroyal agreement resulted in a coin flip to determine ownership. Dinny Phipps got the first foal, the filly named The Bride, and the Chenerys got the second foal, the force named Secretariat.

Dinny's sister Cynthia reaped lasting rewards from the arrangement for outside mares. In 1968 she and Calumet Farm joined in the dual seasons plan to breed Bold Ruler to Calumet's Ponder mare Plum Cake, a stakes winner from the great champion Real Delight. From the first year, Calumet got the Juvenile and National Stallion stakes winner Plum Bold, later an important sire in South Africa. The next year Cynthia got the filly Yule Log. Under the registration procedures of the day, The Jockey Club regarded the owner of the mare at the time of foaling as always the breeder, so records showed the seeming anomaly of a Phipps racing a Bold Ruler filly that was bred by Calumet Farm. (Today, The Jockey Club rules surrounding leases and foal-sharing situations recognize the terms of the specific agreement in determining the breeder, or co-breeders, of record.)

Yule Log was a nice winner, and then produced for Cynthia Phipps the champion Christmas Past (a gray filly by Grey Dawn II). In 1982 Christmas Past's Eclipse Award-winning campaign bespoke family history in

many ways when her owner led her in after the CCA Oaks, carrying old Wheatley silks. Mrs. Phipps' gray High Voltage had won the race in 1955.

Cynthia Phipps recalled that the timing of the onset and treatment of the cancer that would lead to Bold Ruler's death in 1971 was such that she was not prevented from extending the arrangement with Calumet for another two years. From those two years, Calumet got a winner, and Cynthia got Sugar Plum Time, a "Calumet-bred" Bold Ruler filly who won the Firenze and Maskette and one other stakes. Sugar Plum Time foaled the stakes winner Christmas Bonus, who was sold and who foaled the dam of Grand Slam, a Champagne Stakes winner and a leading young stallion as of 2005.

In 1971 Cynthia entered into an arrangement with Hal Price Headley to breed the stakes winner Sari's Song to Bold Ruler. The mare died foaling and, then, Bold Ruler also died, so there would be only one foal. "We decided to race the colt together," Cynthia recalled. Named Singh, the Bold Ruler—Sari's Song colt won the 1975 Jersey Derby and several other stakes.

CHAPTER 12

Sire Of Sires?

Because the separate designs of Nature and the Turf provide that a stallion is represented by runners only three years after his own retirement, it does not take many seasons before a hot sire of racehorses begins to be assessed for his prowess as a sire of sires. In Bold Ruler's case the early returns were spectacular, but most of the sire line faded quickly. While the male line is still a force today — largely via the branch including Seattle Slew and A.P. Indy — there was a time when breeders might have envisioned as expansive a male-line legacy as those subsequently tracing from Northern Dancer and Raise a Native.

In 1970, a year before Bold Ruler's death, his son Cornish Prince debuted on the juvenile sire list, in fourth place. That was the first of fourteen consecutive years that at least one son of Bold Ruler was among the top ten sires of juvenile earners. Five times in that sequence, a son of Bold Ruler led the list: What a Pleasure in 1974 and 1975; Raja Baba in 1976; Secretariat in 1978; and Raja Baba again in 1980. Bold Ruler was still a force, too, and led the list himself in 1972. The apogee of this influence came in 1975, when five of the top ten sires of juvenile earners were sons of Bold Ruler (including leader What a Pleasure).

The impact of Bold Ruler's sons on the general sire list was also significant but not as gaudy. He first had a son on the general list in 1974, the year after his own last season as leading sire. Bold Bidder was second that year, and then What a Pleasure, who stood in Florida, led in 1975–76. In 1979, when Spectacular Bid won the Derby, Preakness, etc., Bold Bidder ranked second. A year later the workmanlike Raja Baba, who stood at Hermitage Farm in Kentucky, rose to first on the general sire list, becoming the second son of Bold Ruler to earn that distinction. Raja Baba also led the juvenile sire list that year. The long life of Raja Baba saw him rising again to ninth on the sire list as late as 1986. This was two years after Triple Crown winner Seattle Slew led the list, he being a great-grandson of Bold Ruler.

Seattle Slew traced to Boldnesian, a Bold Ruler colt whose dam, Alanesian, had been a star filly for William Haggin Perry before he struck his deal with Claiborne. Boldnesian won the 1966 Santa Anita Derby for Perry, but injury ended the colt's apparent classics potential and he went to stud at Dr. William O. Reed's Mare Haven Farm in Florida. (Dr. Reed had veterinary clinics near Hialeah and Belmont Park and was the same veterinarian who had administered the encephalitis shot to Bold Ruler the previous decade.)

Boldnesian sired stakes winner Bold Reasoning, who was bred in Florida by Leon Savage and was sold for only $15,500 at a two-year-olds in training sale. Bold Reasoning raced for Kosgrove Stable, and his victories in the Withers Stakes and Jersey Derby got a foot in the door at Claiborne Farm. He was not a towering success at stud, but he did sire Seattle Slew.

Today the potency of the Bold Ruler sire line seems to depend upon the ongoing influence of the Seattle Slew branch. Seattle Slew's sons who are themselves sires of distinguished males are led by A.P. Indy — in turn the sire of Pulpit, Mineshaft, Golden Missile, Stephen Got Even — while other sons of Slew include

Capote and General Meeting. Boldnesian also got the champion Canadian stallion Bold Ruckus.

The Bold Ruler sire line has lingered into the twenty-first century through other branches as well, including Yes It's True and Notebook, both of whose sire legacy traces through Bold Ruler's son Raja Baba; Fit to Fight, New York Handicap Triple Crown winner and son of Bold Ruler's son Chieftain; Mecke, tracing in male line to What a Pleasure; Tour d'Or, tracing to Secretariat; and Glitterman, a son of Bold Ruler's son Dewan who has accounted for the likes of Balto Star and Glitter Woman.

In earlier years, highlights for sons of Bold Ruler include the American Bold Lad's siring high-class European fillies Marble Arch and Bold Fascinator and the internationalist Sirlad; Chieftain's siring Fit to Fight, plus champion Cascapedia and Kentucky Oaks winner Lucky Lucky Lucky; Bold Hour's siring Travers winner Willow Hour and All Rainbows, dam of Kentucky Derby-winning filly Winning Colors; Bold and Brave's siring Hall of Famer Bold 'n Determined; Top Command's siring filly champion Mom's Command; the consistent Blade getting fifty-one stakes winners; and Jacinto getting thirty-seven stakes winners, including Peacefully, the dam of Kentucky Derby winner Gato Del Sol.

Bold Ruler's greatest son as a racehorse, Secretariat, was a very good stallion who begot champions Lady's Secret and Risen Star. Prominent ongoing presence of Secretariat in pedigrees, however, seems likely to stem from the excellent producing qualities of his daughters.

One of the brilliant sons of Bold Ruler who left a stamp in the stud — but one not blessed with longevity — was Reviewer. Foaled from the Phipps stakes winner Broadway, Reviewer won nine of thirteen starts and earned $247,223, and the Phipps-Hancock consortium concluded he deserved a chance as a Claiborne stallion.

Reviewer was destined to sire the great filly Ruffian, the mention of whose name leads us to another aspect of the Phipps family. Barbara Phipps, one of Mr. and Mrs. Henry Carnegie Phipps' daughters, married Stuart Janney Jr., one of those robust Maryland fellows who place the Maryland Hunt Cup near the top of life's personal goals. Janney merged a successful law career with four victories as a Maryland Hunt Cup jockey.

By the 1950s, Janney once told us, he and his wife were amenable to thinking about breeding horses for

the flat, and their son Stuart III verified in 2005 that the mares they acquired from Mrs. Phipps were fundamental to their involvement and success in that sphere. Stuart III, present chairman of the family's Bessemer Trust and a former chairman of the Thoroughbred Owners and Breeders Association, went so far as to say that he personally might not even be involved in Thoroughbred racing and breeding without that input.

Among the mares the Janneys acquired from Mrs. Phipps was Bold Irish, who in due course foaled the Native Dancer filly Shenanigans. It was Shenanigans who foaled the Janneys' great homebred, Ruffian, to the cover of Reviewer.

Ruffian, of course, was the nonpareil among fillies. She was the unbeaten juvenile filly champion of 1974 and swept the 1975 New York Filly Triple Tiara while still unbeaten. Then, in a match race with another grandchild of Bold Ruler, Foolish Pleasure, she took a misstep and was injured so severely that she could not be saved. (The next year, Reviewer's daughter Revidere, racing for William Haggin Perry, became the sire's second consecutive three-year-old filly champion.)

EPILOGUE

Death Of The Ruler

Bold Ruler was sixteen in 1970 — with many glories behind but the likes of son Secretariat and granddaughter Ruffian as yet unimagined. That year the succulent and nurturing pastures of Claiborne Farm suddenly were disquieted. In July, Bold Ruler's attentive handlers thought they discerned difficulty in his breathing.

"I was coming back from my grandmother's funeral and telephoned the chief of security here at the farm to see if all was well," Claiborne veterinarian Walter Kaufman said. "The chief, Jack McKensie, said I had better have a look at Bold Ruler, that he was making a funny, wheezing sound."

Under close watch the condition seemed to worsen, and farm veterinarians were quick to call in help from among the coterie of vet experts of Central Kentucky.

Ego was not at work here, just the determination to take the best care of a horse.

The breathing problem worsened and, alarmingly, was next accompanied by bleeding from the nostrils. Dr. Loren Evans was called in from the University of Pennsylvania and, along with Dr. Art Davidson — who had thought himself an unintentional pioneer in surgery when he operated on Bold Lad — performed a tracheotomy on Bold Ruler. As described in *The Blood-Horse* by long-time managing editor Larry Shropshire, "use of a lighted tube [inserted into] the throat revealed inflamed tissue, but did not disclose the cause."

By mid-August attending experts concluded that they should place Bold Ruler under general anesthesia for exploratory surgery. This procedure "revealed a tumorous mass protruding from the upper lining deep in the nasal passage, hanging just below a portion of the brain."

Biopsy of a sliver of this mass tested malignant. Mrs. Phipps and her son were being kept informed, and the key policy was that the animal should not be subjected to suffering. The attending veterinarians felt that the mass might be reached by cobalt treatment, and the owners allowed Bold Ruler to be sent to Auburn University in Alabama.

At Auburn, as happens perhaps more than the horse world recognizes, equine veterinary expertise merged with expertise in human medicine. Dr. Jerry Johnson, associate professor of large animal surgery and medicine, and Dr. Jan Bartels, a radiologist, crossed species-treatment lines to receive help from Dr. James Hicks, head of the department of otolaryngology at the University of Alabama Medical School of Birmingham. Expedited delivery of expensive cobalt destined for "bold ruler" might have seemed to some to suggest a United Nations urgency.

Dr. Kaufman of Claiborne later expressed his appreciation: "Dr. Hicks helped get fresh cobalt for treatments and had an air-conditioned stall built at Auburn University and a trailer provided for the horse's groom. And they did that all between Friday night and Monday morning."

No one involved could refer to any precedent for guidance. Bold Ruler was placed under general anesthesia for each application, but those involved had no textbook to follow. Such matters as the dose, number

of treatments, and interval between treatments had to be done by estimate and judgment.

Bold Ruler was the sort of patient whose demeanor and responses did nothing to impede what his saviors were trying to accomplish. The horse had two prolonged stays at Auburn, according to a dispatch by Associated Press reporter Bob Cooper, during which the ailing stallion submitted to the schedule of treatments every five or six days.

Shropshire quoted Dr. Johnson that "regression of the tumor is evident," and Bold Ruler was returned to Claiborne, although no one involved would be so optimistic as to say anything remotely approaching that the horse was cured or the problem solved.

Mrs. Phipps, at age eighty-seven, died on October 18, 1970, a week after Bold Ruler returned to Claiborne Farm.[1] The human sense of a friend departed and an era ended was a matter for the Hancocks themselves. Others with a hands-on duty to the animals could not allow intrusion on their dedication.

"We didn't treat him any different from last year, although we did have to change his tracheotomy tube every day and had to build a higher fence around his paddock so the tube wouldn't catch on it," Dr. Kaufman was quoted by the Associated Press.

Under close watch Bold Ruler resumed a normal routine of barn to paddock. The next winter he resumed breeding and covered thirty-seven mares. The champion Wajima and other stakes winners Singh, Alpine Lass, Our Hero, and Sugar Plum Time resulted from this bonus season at stud.

Dr. Johnson and selected colleagues from Auburn visited Claiborne several times, and X-ray examinations showed good results. Then, in June, not quite a year since his problems first developed, Bold Ruler began to lose weight although he continued to clean his feed tub. Over the next few weeks Bold Ruler's weight and vigor continued to diminish, and on July 2, a biopsy of neck tissue confirmed the fears that the malignancy had recurred. This returning villainy had produced lesions inside the head, neck, and chest. On July 12, 1971, Bold Ruler was euthanized.

The book of valor was closed.

BOLD RULER's PEDIGREE

BOLD RULER, dark bay colt, 1954	NASRULLAH (GB), b, 1940	Nearco, 1935	Pharos, 1920	Phalaris Scapa Flow
			Nogara, 1928	Havresac II Catnip
		Mumtaz Begum, 1932	Blenheim II, 1927	Blandford Malva
			Mumtaz Mahal, 1921	The Tetrarch Lady Josephine
	MISS DISCO, b, 1944	Discovery, 1931	Display, 1923	Fair Play Cicuta
			Ariadne, 1926	Light Brigade Adrienne
		Outdone, 1936	Pompey, 1923	Sun Briar Cleopatra
			Sweep Out, 1926	Sweep On Dugout

BOLD RULER's RACE RECORD

Bold Ruler — **dkb. c. 1954, by Nasrullah (Nearco)–Miss Disco, by Discovery** — **Lifetime record: 33 23 4 2 $764,204**

Own.– Wheatley Stable
Br.– Wheatley Stable (Ky)
Tr.– J. Fitzsimmons

26Jly58- 6Jam	fst	1 3/16	:471	1:114	1:37	1:553	3↑	Brooklyn H 57k	1	3	37½	51½	78	715	Arcaro E	136wb	*.40	83-15	Cohoes1101[D]Shrpsburg1146½ThrdBrothr110hd	Tired,roughed	8
19Jly58- 6Mth	fst	1¼	:48	1:12	1:362	2:013	3↑	Monmouth H 110k	1	1	11½	1hd	1½	1¾	Arcaro E	134wb	*.30	98-20	BoldRuler134¾Sharpsburg1136Bll'sSkyBoy105¾	Well in hand	6
4Jly58- 6Bel	fst	1¼	:471	1:103	1:351	2:01	3↑	Suburban H 83k	1	3	3nk	11	12	1no	Arcaro E	134wb	*.50	95-11	BoldRuler134noClm1091½ThrdBrothr1101¼	Strong drive,held	8
25Jun58- 6Bel	fst	1⅛	:473	1:111	1:352	1:482	3↑	Stymie H 28k	3	1	12½	12½	16	15	Arcaro E	133wb	*.40	94-18	BoldRuler1335AdmiralVee112¾PopCorn1081¼	Speed to spare	7
14Jun58- 7Bel	fst	1	:231	:461	1:103	1:353	3↑	Metropolitan H 58k	1	1	12	11	11½	22	Arcaro E	135wb	*.95	94-13	GallantMan1302BoldRuler1351½Clm114nk	Tired under impost	10
30May58- 7Bel	fst	7f	:223	:453	1:101	1:223	3↑	Carter H 58k	3	1	41¼	31	11½	11½	Arcaro E	135wb	*.80	94-17	BoldRuler1351½TickTock1131½GllntMn128no	Briskly handled	9
17May58- 7Bel	fst	6f-WC	:22	:443		1:09	3↑	Toboggan H 29k	2	2		3nk	2½	1½	Arcaro E	133wb	*.40	94-08	BoldRuler133½Clem1172TickTock1163	Under strong handling	10
9Nov57- 7GS	gd	1¼	:471	1:111	1:364	2:013	3↑	Trenton H 82k	1	1	18	13½	13	12¼	Arcaro E	122wb	1.60	97-14	BoldRuler1222¼GallantMan1248½RoundTable124	Ridden out	3
2Nov57- 7GS	sly	1 1/16	:231	:462	1:11	1:441		Benjamin Franklin H 27k	4	1	19	111	114	112	Arcaro E	136wb	*.20	89-20	BoldRuler13612Sarno1096JetColonel1132½	Breezing all way	4
19Oct57- 7Jam	fst	1 1/16	:234	:463	1:103	1:424	3↑	Queens County H 28k	1	1	14	16	16	12½	Arcaro E	133wb	*.25	96-15	Bold Ruler1332½Promised Land1113½Greek Spy114½	Eased up	6
9Oct57- 7Bel	sly	7f	:223	:45	1:084	1:212	2↑	Vosburgh H 23k	3	1	2hd	11½	15	19	Arcaro E	130wb	*.40	103-09	BoldRulr1309TckTock117½St.AmourII1141¾	Fast pace,in hand	8
28Sep57- 7Bel	fst	1¼	:471	1:11	1:36	2:01	3↑	Woodward 106k	2	2	21	11	2½	33½	Arcaro E	120wb	2.15	91-13	Dedicate1261½GallantMn1202BoldRulr120hd	Took lead,tired	4
14Sep57- 7Bel	sly	1	:23	:454	1:094	1:35		Jerome H 29k	6	3	3½	11	13	16	Arcaro E	130wb	*.20e	99-07	BoldRuler1306Bureaucracy1131¼WingedMercury1062	In hand	6
9Sep57- 7Bel	fst	6f	:222	:453		1:101		Handicap 15000	1	2	2hd	1hd	14	15½	Arcaro E	128wb	*.85	98-13	BoldRuler1285½GreekGame1215Egotistcl115nk	Scored easily	8
15Jun57- 6Bel	fst	1½	:464	1:102	2:012	2:263		Belmont 113k	1	1	13	1hd	21½	312	Arcaro E	126wb	*.85	93-07	GallantMan1268InsideTract1264BoldRuler1269	Tired badly	6
18May57- 7Pim	fst	1 3/16	:462	1:103	1:363	1:561		Preakness 113k	5	1	11	11½	12	12	Arcaro E	126wb	1.40	92-13	BoldRuler1262IronLiege126nkInsideTrct1262¼	Well handled	7
13May57- 0Pim	fst	1 1/16	:231	:464	1:11	1:433		Alw 6000	3	2	12	1hd	1hd	11	Arcaro E	124wb	-	92-16	Bold Ruler1241Inswept12012Convoy117	No difficulty	3
	Special event between 7th and 8th races - No wagering																				
4May57- 7CD	fst	1¼	:47	1:112	1:364	2:021		Ky Derby 152k	7	2	32	31½	51¼	45¾	Arcaro E	126 w	*1.20	90-12	IronLiege126noGallantMan1262¾RoundTable1263	No excuse	9
20Apr57- 7Jam	fst	1⅛	:48	1:12	1:361	1:484		Wood Memorial 59k	2	1	1½	1hd	2hd	1no	Arcaro E	126 w	*.50	102-10	BoldRuler126noGallantMan1266PromisedLand1262¼	Just up	7
30Mar57- 7GP	fst	1⅛	:462	1:102	1:343	1:464		Fla Derby 123k	1	2	21	21	1hd	21½	Arcaro E	122 w	*.60	107-06	Gen.Duk1221½BoldRulr122hdIronLg1182¼	Reached lead,tired	5
2Mar57- 7Hia	fst	1⅛	:452	1:102	1:342	1:47		Flamingo 131k	2	3	21	11½	12	1nk	Arcaro E	122 w	*.50	101-07	BoldRuler122nkGen.Duke1222¾IronLiege12212	Held gamely	7
16Feb57- 7Hia	fst	1⅛	:462	1:102	1:343	1:472		Everglades 30k	4	1	11½	11½	11	2hd	Arcaro E	126 w	*.40	99-10	Gen.Duke114hdBoldRuler1266IronLg1171¾	Strong try,headed	7
30Jan57- 7Hia	fst	7f	:223	:45	1:091	1:22		Bahamas 26k	2	3	12	11½	14	14½	Atkinson T	126 w	3.85e	100-11	BoldRuler1264½Gen.Duke1142FederalHll1261¼	Scored easily	11
6Nov56- 7Jam	fst	1 1/16	:24	:48	1:13	1:453		©Remsen 96k	5	8	87¼	89	1019	-	Arcaro E	122 w	*.60	- -	Ambhavng1222½Missle1221½Finlandia122nk	Poor start,blocked	11
	Geldings not eligible																				
27Oct56- 7GS	gd	1 1/16	:221	:454	1:12	1:444		Garden State 319k	1	3	33	1724	1734	1724	Atkinson T	122 w	*2.10	62-18	Barbizon122noFederalHill122nkAmrullh1223	Stumbled early	19
13Oct56- 7Bel	fst	6½-WC	:214	:442	1:083	1:151		Futurity 124k	8	2		22	13	12¼	Arcaro E	122 w	*1.25	96-04	BoldRuler1222¼GreekGame122noAmrullh122nk	Under pressure	13
	Geldings not eligible																				
5Oct56- 6Bel	fst	6f-WC	:22	:442		1:083		Sp Wt 7500	7	4		2hd	1hd	1½	Guerin E	118 w	*.90	96-04	BoldRuler118½Missile1182½Mqult118½	Under strong pressure	9
24Sep56- 6Bel	sly	6f-WC	:223	:453		1:101		Alw 5000	1	3		2hd	2hd	21¼	Arcaro E	122 w	*.95e	87-19	Nashville1161¼Bold Ruler1221½Bureaucracy113nk	Bore out	6
6Jun56- 7Bel	fst	5f-WC	:22	:441		:56		Juvenile 33k	1	1		21½	21½	11	Arcaro E	122 w	*.60e	99-05	Bold Ruler1221King Hairan1225Supernatural1225	In hand	8
24May56- 6Bel	fst	5f-WC	:221	:451		:571		Alw 5000	7	4		2hd	1½	1nk	Arcaro E	122 w	*.55e	93-13	Bold Ruler122nkKing Hairan1227Bureaucracy1195	All out	9
2May56- 7Jam	fst	5f	:23	:463		:594		©Youthful 17k	8	6	41	2hd	1hd	13½	Atkinson T	122 w	*1.00e	91-19	Bold Ruler1223½Red Cadet1221½Encore1223½	Well in hand	10
19Apr56- 5Jam	fst	5f	:223	:47		1:00		Alw 4000	4	2	2hd	2hd	2hd	11	Atkinson T	118 w	3.15	90-20	Bold Ruler1181Red Cadet1181¾Missile1181½	Ridden out	8
9Apr56- 4Jam	gd	5f	:232	:474		1:002		©Md Sp Wt	2	3	21½	2hd	11½	13½	Atkinson T	118 w	*1.55	88-15	BoldRuler1183½WolfBadge118½ScotchRoyal1182	Easy score	6

Notes

Chapter 4, p. 44

1. A strange statistical practice abetted Nasrullah's leading the sire list in England in 1951. That year, one of the key races in England, the King George VI and Queen Elizabeth Stakes, was won by Supreme Court. This colt was foaled from a mare that had been covered by two stallions the previous year — Persian Gulf and Precipitation. Both stallions were denied credit for Supreme Court's earnings by the way statistics were gathered; otherwise, either would have had higher progeny earnings than Nasrullah.

Chapter 7, p. 101

1. In later years the practice of running a pacemaker came to be referred to as using a "rabbit." Ironically, Nerud was on the opposite side of the scenario with his great 1960s front-runner Dr. Fager. Frank Whiteley several times employed Hedevar as the "rabbit" for Dr. Fager's archrival Damascus, and in the climactic 1967 Woodward Stakes, the Phipps stables used Great Power as an additional "rabbit" for champion Buckpasser. The strategy worked, as Damascus won from Buckpasser with Dr. Fager third.

Chapter 8, p. 121

1. Mrs. Phipps' grandson Dinny said that a few years later, his grandmother acquired a helicopter for the primary purpose of attending her horses' out-of-town races. His aunt, Mrs. Sonia Seherr-Thoss, expanded this memory to say Mrs. Phipps also used the chopper for quick trips from Palm Beach to Lake Okeechobee for quail hunting.

Chapter 10, p. 146

1. We presume Mr. Hatton had in mind the compliment that Belmont Park management did not scrape, drag, or otherwise manage the racing strip so as to induce impressive times in important races. The irony of the comment springs from the oft-repeated doubt about Whisk Broom II's record of 2:00 when he won the 1913 Suburban at Belmont. Despite skepticism this record was recognized officially as unmatched until Kelso tied it in an age of more impeccable chronometry, in the 1961 Woodward.

Chapter 11

1. (p. 163) Bold Ruler and Round Table looked across the aisle at each other in the Claiborne stallion barn for a number of years.

2. (p. 168) In the author's one opportunity to have a conversation — we recall it more as an "audience" — with Mr. Fitzsimmons, we were seated in lawn chairs near the paddock at Hialeah. It was the year Bold Lad — in the first crop Mr. Fitz had not had his hands on — was being prepared to come back for his three-year-old season. The old gentleman still paid close attention to the stable, and he remarked that, "The one I like for later on is Bold Bidder," in reference to another of Mrs. Phipps' Bold Ruler three-year-olds. Well, "later on" got later and later and Bold Bidder still had not distinguished himself.

Dinny Phipps recalled that, "I walked into the barn one day and my grandmother was saying she wanted to sell Bold Bidder. I said that I'd like to buy him, and she answered, 'If I wanted you to buy him, I'd give him to you.' " Bold Bidder was instead sold to Paul Falkenstein, not long before he blossomed to win the Jerome and two other stakes. Falkenstein cashed in before the year was out, selling the colt on to a high-powered partnership of John Gaines, John Hanes, and John Olin. They placed him in the care of trainer Woody Stephens, and Bold Bidder became the champion older horse of 1966. Mr. Fitz had been right on the money. As mentioned elsewhere, Bold Bidder became an important sire as well.

Epilogue, p. 183

1. Many transitions were imposed on the players of this drama within a short time. Bull Hancock of Claiborne Farm died in 1972, but after a period of reorganization, his young son Seth took the helm and his older son Arthur III established his own farm. Both have succeeded in the intervening three decades. Ogden Phipps lived until 2000, and son Dinny and daughter Cynthia have continued the family tradition and the connection with Claiborne Farm. Mrs. A.B. Hancock Jr. survived her husband by more than thirty years, then passed away in 2005.

Index

Photo Credits

Cover photo: (Keeneland-Morgan Collection)

Page 1: Bold Ruler conformation (The Blood-Horse); Bold Ruler at Pimlico (The Blood-Horse)

Page 2: Nearco (British Racehorse); Nasrullah (Skeets Meadors); Miss Disco (Bert Morgan/NYRA); Discovery (The Blood-Horse)

Page 3: Mrs. Gladys Phipps (Hugh Miller); Mrs. Phipps with Bold Ruler (Mike Sirico/NYRA); Eddie Arcaro (Bert Morgan/NYRA)

Page 4: Sunny Jim Fitzsimmons with Bold Ruler (Bert Morgan/NYRA); Bold Ruler going for a workout (Skeets Meadors)

Page 5: The Youthful winner's circle (Bert and Richard Morgan); Winning the Juvenile (Bert Morgan); Winning the Futurity (Mike Sirico/NYRA)

Page 6: Winning the Bahamas (The Blood-Horse); Winning the Flamingo (The Blood-Horse); Wood Memorial winner's circle (The Blood-Horse)

Page 7: Winning the Preakness (Jerry Frutkoff); Preakness winner's circle (Baltimore Sun); Trophy presentation (Jerry Frutkoff)

Page 8: Winning the Times Square (Bert and Richard Morgan); Winning the Jerome (Bert and Richard Morgan); Winning the Benjamin Franklin Handicap (Turfotos)

Page 9: Winning the Trenton (Turfotos); Bold Ruler working (Bert and Richard Morgan); Bold Ruler, Nov. 1957 (The Blood-Horse)

Page 10-11: Winning the Toboggan (Bert and Richard Morgan); Winning the Carter (Bert and Richard Morgan); Winning the Stymie (both, Bert and Richard Morgan)

Page 12: Winning the Suburban (Bert and Richard Morgan); Monmouth winner's circle (Turfotos)

Page 13: Bold Ruler at Claiborne (The Blood-Horse); Bold Ruler in front of white stallion barn (Skeets Meadors)

Page 14: Bold Bidder (Allen F. Brewer Jr.); Secretariat (Tony Leonard); Bold Lad (J. Noye); Irish-bred Bold Lad (Bobby Hopkins); Wajima (Jim Raftery)

Page 15: Lamb Chop (Turfotos); Queen Empress (Turfotos); Queen of the Stage (Turfotos); Gamely (Hollywood Park)

Page 16: Bold Ruler in paddock (J. Noye); Gravestone (Barbara D. Livingston)

ABOUT THE AUTHOR

Edward L. Bowen is considered one of Thoroughbred racing's most insightful and erudite writers. A native of West Virginia, Bowen grew up in South Florida, where he became enamored of racing while watching televised stakes from Hialeah.

Bowen entered journalism school at the University of Florida in 1960, then transferred to the University of Kentucky in 1963 so he could work as a writer for *The Blood-Horse*, the leading weekly Thoroughbred magazine. From 1968 to 1970, he served as editor of *The Canadian Horse*, then returned to *The Blood-Horse* as managing editor. He rose to the position of editor-in-chief before leaving the publication in 1993.

Bowen is president of the Grayson-Jockey Club Research Foundation, which raises funds for equine research. In addition to *Bold Ruler*, Bowen is the author of sixteen other books, including *Belmont Park: A Century of Champions*, *Man o' War*, *At the Wire: Horse Racing's Greatest Moments*, and the two-volume set, *Legacies of the Turf*. Bowen has won the Eclipse Award for magazine writing as well as other writing awards. He lives in Versailles, Kentucky, with his wife, Ruthie, and son, George. Bowen has two grown daughters, Tracy Bowen and Jennifer Schafhauser, and two grandchildren.

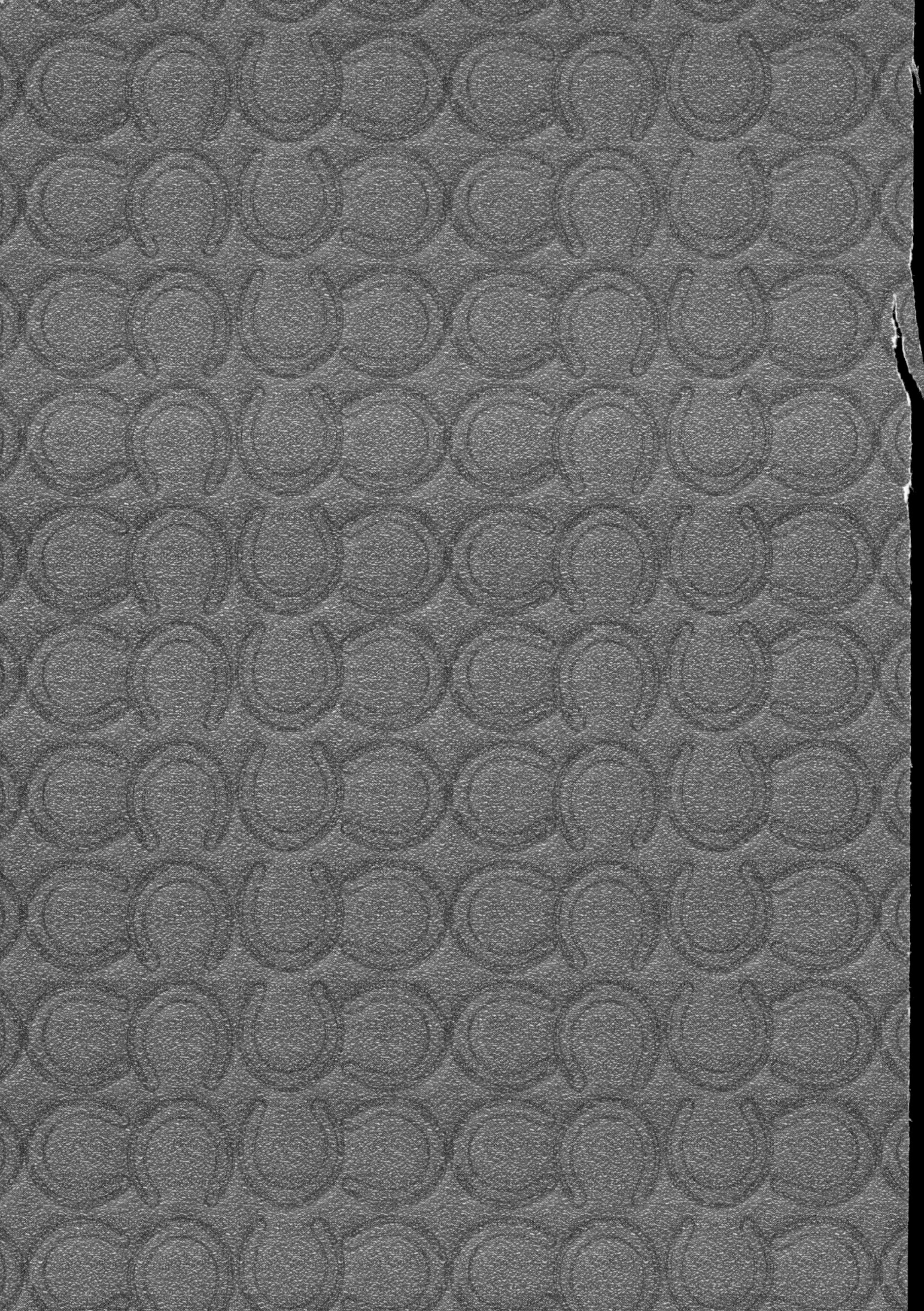